CREATED EQUAL

CREATED EQUAL

the lives and ideas of black american innovators

JAMES MICHAEL BRODIE

WILLIAM MORROW AND COMPANY, INC.

NEW YORK

Library of Congress Cataloging-in-Publication Data

Brodie, James Michael, 1957–
    Created equal : the lives and ideas of Black American innovators /
James Michael Brodie.
        p.   cm.
    Includes index.
    ISBN 0-688-11536-5
    1. Afro-Americans—Biography.   2. Afro-American inventors—
Biography.   3. Afro-American scientists—Biography.   I. Title.
E185.96.B835   1993
509.2'273—dc20
    [B]   92-40979
                                                            CIP

Printed in the United States of America

First Edition

1 2 3 4 5 6 7 8 9 10

BOOK DESIGN BY LISA STOKES

This was perhaps the easiest part of this entire project. To my mother, Alberta B. K. Brodie, who gave me my life; to my sister, Vicki L. Brodie, who was there when I needed her; to my brother, Phillip K. Brodie, who believed in me when I did not; and to my father, James A. Brodie, who, despite our disagreements, has always been my hero.
A special thank you and a special prayer also go out to Frank Phillips, wherever you may be. From you I learned much. I only wish you were here on earth to share this.

PREFACE

The creativity of African people was evident long before they were brought to the North American continent. European explorers were in awe over the advancement of African civilizations, and they returned home with wondrous stories of a black-skinned people who were more advanced in their knowledge of astronomy, navigation, mathematics, architecture, literature, and agriculture than anyone they had ever encountered.

They spoke of the mighty empires, the power and emotion in the art, the elaborate governments and ornate cities, the detailed codes of law, and the ingenious methods Africans used to irrigate their crops, keep time, and embalm their dead. In fact, the first noted European historian and philosopher Herodotus, a Greek, remarked in the fifth century B.C. that Africa was the greatest civilization in human history.

Throughout history hundreds of inventors and pioneers of African origin have made their indelible mark on the world.

Preface

But as more and more African contributions found their way into emerging European civilizations, fewer wound up in the annals of Western history. In *Created Equal*, James Michael Brodie, a respected journalist and education writer, excavates more of the artifacts of African American genius. This book, like others before it, reminds readers that the concept of creativity is not a Western phenomenon but a human one.

It also says something significant about the strength of a people who, despite denial of their intelligence and repression of their ingenuity, went on to develop some of humanity's greatest gifts. From Alabama Vest's kazoo to Dr. Earl Shaw's spin-flip, tunable laser (which made it possible to control the intensity of the beam needed in intricate microsurgery), the range of African American creativity knows no bounds.

In *The Souls of Black Folk*, W.E.B. Du Bois reminded his audience that the "color line" was the boundary that would stymie African American ascension. In this book Mr. Brodie reminds *his* audience that neither lynchings nor the law will ever again deny African Americans their deserved recognition.

—Ed Wiley III
Associate Editor,
Black Issues in Higher Education

ACKNOWLEDGMENTS

To: Donna Barne, Esmeralda Barnes, Susan Blake, Walter Blake, Charles Blockson, Lovette Clark, Tim Clark, Victoria Coleman, Dorothea Colvin, Jacqueline Conciatore, Barbara Egypt, Carol Drake Friedman, Marc Jenkins, Manny Jefferson, Don Johnson, William King, Graene Littler, Joye Mercer, Michael Poindexter, William Pitts, Beth Pratt-Dewey, Roberto Rodriguez, James K. Salsberry III, Wilfred Samuels, Eric Shimizu, Ward Shimizu, George Walker, Ian Walker, Constance Williams, Ed Wiley, Ed Wiley III, and the Brodie and Knight families.

CONTENTS

Contents

Contents

INTRODUCTION

Understanding the contributions made by African inventors and scientists in the Western Hemisphere is impossible without recognizing the conditions under which they created. Each innovator, in her or his search to solve a particular dilemma, made her or his discoveries in the face of an often hateful and indifferent society.

From the very outset of expansion into the Americas, the inventiveness and labor of Africans play an integral role. The Black presence in America dates at least as far back as Columbus's expedition in 1492, when Pedro Alonso Niño—described by historians as "Negro"—piloted one of the three ships to what is now known as America. In 1513 Vasco Núñez de Balboa sailed to the Pacific with a crew that included thirty Africans.

In 1527 a Moroccan named Esteban—also known as Estevanico and Stephan Dorantez—led an expedition from Sanlúcas de Barrameda, Spain, to the American West, into what are now the states of Arizona and New Mexico. Esteban was part of the westward European journey through the Americas in search of gold and other riches. He was killed in 1539 as he attempted to explore Zuñi territory in what is now New Mexico.

The year 1619 signaled the beginning of European expansion into the "New World." It also marked the beginning of the African slave trade across the Atlantic. In August twenty Africans were brought over as indentured servants to the new Jamestown, Virginia, settlement aboard a Dutch ship. In 1624 William Tucker was born in captivity at Jamestown, becoming the first African to be stripped of his traditional tribal name.

It should be noted here that while the actual taking of Africans into slavery may have begun in 1441, when ten Africans were delivered to Prince Henry of Portugal, for the purposes of this book, we refer to the transatlantic trade.

Massachusetts was the first state to recognize slavery in its Body of Liberties in 1641. Such famed landmarks as the House of Seven Gables in Salem, Massachusetts, were major headquarters for that state's deadly trade. Africans owned by Captain John Turner, brought to Salem as cargo via Turner's dealings in Barbados, lived in the house. It wasn't until February 1992 that historians for the Salem house publicly acknowledged the role the building played in the slave trade.

Profits from slave commerce were used to finance the textile revolution in Massachusetts and Rhode Island. During the middle 1860s southern slaves produced 80 percent of the world's supply of raw cotton, much of which was used in New England textile mills.

In 1642 Virginia passed a statute making slavery hereditary, passed along through the mother's line. This allowed slaveowners to bed their female chattel without worrying over the messy details of what to do with the progeny. Three years later Maryland passed a law forbidding the marriage of White women to African men. By 1671 that state's slavery laws were further toughened to preclude Africans from converting to Christianity as a path to salvation and freedom. Apparently, some Africans had been able to claim freedom based on religious conversion.

A 1705 Virginia law allowed slaveowners to list Africans as property. The law's full intent was not realized until July 1776, when the Declaration of Independence was ratified, and later, through compromises in the Constitution. These compromises allowed states to increase their representation in Congress by counting each slave as three fifths of a citizen. The slaves were not afforded any voting power and had no political rights.

The denial of basic human and spiritual rights to Africans made easier the later stripping away of other rights and dignities. How could people with no identity, for example, carry patents in their names?

Contrary to popular belief, Thomas L. Jennings, not Henry Blair, was the first Black to receive a patent, on March 3, 1821—thirteen years ahead of Blair. Jennings's patent was for a dry-cleaning process. He used the money he earned to purchase his family out of slavery.

The 1790 U.S. Patent Act should have opened the door to free Black inventors. Despite this, few of them even attempted to patent their creations. Enslaved Blacks had even fewer options. Until 1858 slavery laws made the inventions of slaves the property of their enslavers. It may never be known just how many inventions credited to Whites were actually created by their African captives.

The real name or even minute details of the life of a slave called Ned might never have been known save for the greed of his slaver. Ned invented a cotton harvester. His machine was so efficient and laborsaving that his master, O.J.E. Stuart of Pike County, Mississippi, attempted to get the invention patented in his own name in 1857. Stuart argued that since he owned Ned, he owned anything created by Ned.

The Reconstruction era saw a burst of patents filed by Black inventors. Between 1871 and 1900 more than three hundred patents were awarded to Blacks.

Introduction

Because of the menial position Africans held in society, most of the inventions served domestic needs, such as farm and kitchen utensils, trouser leg straighteners, cosmetic products, and Sarah Boone's ironing board. Then there was Thomas, credited with making the first potato chip while he was a chef in Saratoga Springs, New York, sometime during the 1800s. And before S. R. Scottron invented it in 1892, there was no such thing as a curtain rod.

Other inventions were unusual contraptions, such as Marjorie Joyner's 1928 permanent wave machine, which more closely resembled a ghoulish horror-movie torture machine and may have been about the last thing any woman would want plugged in and attached to her head. Other inventions were garish and grisly weapons, such as Louis Temple's toggle-blade harpoon, which was designed to lock itself into a whale's flesh.

Black innovators, such as Garrett A. Morgan, peanut exponent and chemist George Washington Carver, and Lewis Latimer are fairly well known, but many other inventors have long since fallen into obscurity, regardless of the importance of their contributions. Some, such as blood bank pioneer Charles Drew, heart surgeon Daniel Hale Williams, and cell biologist Ernest Just, are not even mentioned in scientific books featuring their contemporaries.

Even when their breakthroughs proved beneficial to society as a whole, Black inventors were shunned by bigoted Whites. For example, to sell his brand-new "breathing device"—the precursor to the gas mask—in the early 1900s, Morgan pretended not only that he was not its inventor, but that he was not Black. Realizing that Whites would not accept the device if they thought a Black man had created it, he posed as a Native American, traveling with a white assistant who was credited with the invention.

Aside from Carver, Black innovators weren't immortalized in the movies. How would the big screen have treated Howard St. Clair Jones, Jr., who holds thirty-one patents in the field of microwave technology, or J. H. Dickenson, who garnered a dozen patents for adjustments to the player piano during the 1800s?

Almost lost in time are John P. Parker, who in 1884 patented a screw for a tobacco press, and Frederick M. Johnson, who in 1912 invented a self-feeding rifle that could fire three hundred shots at a rate of twenty a second.

One wonders what kind of doctor Elizabeth Singleton would have made had she been given the chance. The Tennessee midwife delivered more than a thousand babies during the 1800s and lived to the ripe age of a hundred and four. Would the name Henry Creamer, holder of seven patents for the steam trap during the 1800s, be on the lips of every citizen? How would movies about the Old West have been different if Baz Reeves—the real "Lone Ranger"—had been accurately depicted?

Through all the pain, and perhaps because of it, African creativity found outlets, and we in turn are the better for it.

CREATED EQUAL

SLAVE INVENTORS

Ned, 1800s

Ned was a slave on the plantation of Oscar J. E. Stuart in Pike County, Mississippi, who on August 25, 1857, wrote to Secretary of the Interior Jacob Thompson regarding a cotton scraper Ned had invented. The device required one person and two horses and could do the work of four people, four horses, two scrapers, and two plows. Stuart argued in his letter to Thompson that ownership of the machine was rightfully his, explaining that "the master is the owner of the fruits of the labor of the slave both intiliectual [*sic*] and manual."

Stuart appealed to the sensibilities of Thompson, also a southerner, rather than approach Joseph Holt, the commissioner of patents, who was a northerner. Thompson, however, referred the case to Attorney General Jeremiah Black.

Stuart then wrote to Holt and included a document signed by Ned declaring that the African was indeed the inventor and that he belonged to Stuart. Stuart explained: "The affidavit of the Negro I regarded as a matter of supererogation, mere surplussage [*sic*], neither strengthening or diminishing whatever merits there might be in my application."

But Holt ruled that since Ned was not a citizen, he could not file a patent request. This drew an angry response from Stuart. "I was never such an unmitigated fool which is the implication of the act of the Commissioner as to imagine that a slave could obtain a patent for a useful invention when under the laws, it is a question . . . whether the master who has the property alike in the fruits of the mind and labor."

Stuart assured Holt that if his slave were to try patenting the invention on his own, "for such impertinence, you know according to our southern usage, I would correct him."

Holt ruled on June 10, 1858, that "a machine invented by a slave, though it be new and useful, cannot, in the present state of the law, be patented. I may add that if such a patent were issued to the master, it would not protect him in the courts against persons who might infringe it." The ruling stood until after the Civil War, when it was overturned by the ratification of the Thirteenth and Fourteenth amendments, which abolished slavery and then established "equal protection" and "due process" for Blacks.

By 1860 Stuart had begun marketing Ned's creation. In a broadside advertisement for the machine was a letter of support to Stuart from A. G. Brown, a planter: "I am glad to know that your implement is the invention of a negro slave—thus giving the lie to the abolition cry that slavery dwarfs the mind of the negro. When did a free negro ever invent anything?" Angered over what he referred to as the "excesses" of Reconstruction, Stuart eventually left Mississippi. It is not known what became of Ned.

Jo Anderson, ca. 1800s

Cyrus McCormick, known for the invention of the automatic reaper, apparently gave a great deal of credit for the invention to Jo Anderson, a slave on his plantation. There also is some evidence that suggests that McCormick may not have been the true inventor at all, that his wife may have been the machine's real creator.

Wilcie Elfe, 1800s

Elfe was a slave pharmacist in South Carolina. According to some accounts, he kept a prescription book, last dated 1853, in which he outlined several drugs he created. Apparently Elfe also sold his concoctions, though little is known about those creations.

Onesimus, 1700s

Onesimus was the property of the Puritan leader Cotton Mather. In 1721 Onesimus developed a cure for the smallpox virus—a highly contagious, often fatal disease that causes high fever and severe skin eruptions—which was rampant throughout New England.

Onesimus never received credit for his discovery, which he told Mather was a common remedy in Africa. Mather sent the serum to a Dr. Boylston, who tried it out on his son and two slaves. Claiming the drug as his own, Boylston was honored with a fellowship by the Royal Society of London.

Near the end of the eighteenth century Edward Jenner found that the cowpox virus was an effective vaccine against smallpox. It is not known whether Jenner knew of Onesimus. Today the disease is virtually nonexistent.

Anthony Weston, 1800s

Weston was a slave of Benjamin Hunt of Charleston, South Carolina. In 1831 Weston made improvements to W. T. Catto's threshing machine. Hunt received the patent and made a tidy sum from the sale of the improved machine.

Perhaps Hunt was able to get his patent because, unlike Oscar J. E. Stuart of Mississippi, he did not divulge the identity of the true inventor.

Henry Boyd, 1802–1866

Henry Boyd used his carpentry skills and one invention to buy himself and his family out of slavery. His invention, the Boyd bedstead, was constructed in such a way that its wooden bed rails could be screwed into both the headboard and the footboard, creating a stronger structure.

Boyd was born into slavery in Kentucky in 1802. At a young age he was apprenticed to a cabinetmaker. He began saving his money, hoping to earn enough to buy his freedom. Armed with a general pass from his slaver, he went to work in the Kanawaha saltworks, working double time for double pay. He cut wood by day and tended to a boiling salt kettle by night until he had saved enough.

Many Black carpenters used their skills to escape bondage. They knew, for example, that cabinetmakers were afforded a higher status and were more in demand than general carpenters, so they sought out that skill.

A free man in 1826, Boyd went to Cincinnati to seek his fortune. What he encountered were shop owners who would not hire a Black man. He took jobs as a laborer and bided his time.

He eventually teamed with a White carpenter and began building houses. He soon earned enough to purchase his brother and sister. By 1833 Boyd was worth more than three thousand dollars. Three years later he opened his own company, using his bed frame design as its foundation. Boyd never received a patent for his bed design, though he did try to have it protected by having a White man apply for the patent.

To ensure that his customers were getting the real thing,

Boyd stamped his name on every frame he made. By 1843 he was among Cincinnati's most successful furniture makers. He had a staff of twenty-five to fifty employees and owned steam-powered machines. The majority of his customers seemed to come from the South and the ever-expanding Southwest.

Twice Boyd's plant was torched by arsonists. Twice, thanks to insurance, he rebuilt. But in 1863, when no insurance company would insure his business because of the risk, he retired. He died three years later.

Benjamin Bradley, 1840–?

Around 1856 Bradley, a slave, constructed a working model of a steam engine, using two round pieces of steel, a gun barrel, and pewter. He also constructed an engine powerful enough to run a small boat. Though unable to read or write, Bradley worked as a laboratory technician at the United States Naval Academy in Annapolis, Maryland. His duties included preparing experiments for class study.

EARLY INNOVATORS

Benjamin Banneker, 1731–1806

Her name was Anola. Benjamin Banneker was twenty-eight and very much in love with her. They planned to get married. But Anola belonged to a Maryland slaveowner who refused to grant her freedom or to sell her to Banneker. Undaunted, the man who later planned the nation's capital devised a scheme to steal her away and had booked passage for them on a ship bound for England. Little is known of the daring rescue attempt except that it failed. At least one Banneker biographer claimed Anola later committed suicide by drowning herself. While the idea is wonderfully romantic and seems to explain a relatively unknown aspect of the scientist's life, it unfortunately never happened. The truth is there is not a lot of information about Banneker's private life. In the void a number of tales were born, with a few documented.

SURVEYOR OF A CAPITAL

In 1791 Banneker was appointed to a three-man team of surveyors named by President George Washington to design the District of Columbia. He was the first African to receive a presidential appointment. Banneker took over the project when Major Pierre Charles L'Enfant, chairman of the three-man civil engineering team, resigned and returned to Paris, taking the plans with him. Banneker reproduced the plans from memory, some historians say.

In 1991 a committee formed to push for a Banneker statue in Washington was accused of overstating the mathematician's role in shaping the city by saying that it was Banneker who completed L'Enfant's design. Others believe that Major Andrew Ellicott—the third man—completed L'Enfant's design. That Banneker played a prominent role is unquestioned. The extent of that role remains the subject of dispute.

DESCENDANT OF BANNEKA

Banneker was born in 1731 to a free mulatto mother and an African father who had purchased his way out of slavery. In 1737 the Bannekers had saved enough to buy a 102-acre farm along the Patapsco River, about 10 miles from Baltimore. The elder Banneker paid seventeen thousand pounds of tobacco for the land, which became well known for its vegetables, fruit, poultry goods, and honey.

Robert—Benjamin's father and a native of Guiana, West Africa—was awarded his freedom after converting to the Christian faith in Maryland, despite that state's law prohibiting freedom for Blacks on such grounds. When Robert wed Mary Banneker, he took her name, having no name of his own to give to her.

Mary Banneker—Benjamin's mother—was one of four freeborn daughters of a woman named Molly Welsh, a White English milkmaid, who took advantage of a loophole in the law to escape being hanged for stealing a pail of milk from her employer. Instead, in 1683, Welsh was exiled to America. She settled in Maryland. By 1690 she had paid off the cost of her overseas trip by working as an indentured servant. Suddenly a free woman, with nothing to her name but an ox, a gun, two hoes, and the clothes on her back, Welsh worked on various farms along the Patapsco River and soon earned enough to buy her own land and two slaves.

One of the servants, an African prince named Banneka, refused to do menial tasks for his new mistress. Eventually she freed both slaves and married Banneka. Molly ignored the accepted custom by allowing Banneka to retain his true name and even assuming it when they married. She also took on a considerable risk by intermarrying, which could have meant enslavement for the White woman under emerging laws.

The original Banneka name was misspelled first to Banneky and eventually to its modern form.

A YOUNG CURIOSITY

Benjamin Banneker spent most of his young life on the farm, going off to a Quaker school only during the winter. He attended integrated private schools, where he devoted more of his time to reading than playing with the other children. He had the equivalent of an eighth-grade education by the time he was fifteen, with much of what he knew coming from his grandmother, Molly, who taught him to read. Eventually he took over operation of the family farm.

Historians point to two events as critical in the development of Banneker's intellectual growth. The first event was a gift of a pocket watch from a traveling salesman named Josef Levi. The watch was unlike anything young Banneker had ever seen and was his first real exposure to the wonders of technology.

For weeks the pocket watch occupied him, as he took it apart and reassembled it to understand better the gadget's inner workings. By 1752, using the watch as a guide, he had built his own wooden clock—the first such in what was later the United

31

States. Each gear, each movement, and each chime were hand-carved, with additional parts coming from wherever he could find them. The clock, which became something of a curiosity in the region, lasted some forty years.

Banneker also had become a curiosity. News spread about this young genius, excellent with numbers, knowledgeable about the weather, mechanics, and farming. People came from neighboring towns to meet him and quiz him.

By 1759 both Banneker's father and grandmother had died. His three sisters had married and moved away, leaving Benjamin and his mother alone to run the farm. For nineteen years he had to shelve his scientific interests.

In 1772 Andrew Ellicott moved to the area from Bucks County, Pennsylvania, with his three sons to build their mill. The fast friendship between Banneker and the Quaker family is seen by Banneker biographers as the second significant event in his life.

Ellicott believed that tobacco—the area's chief and only crop—was destroying the land and convinced farmers to grow wheat in its place. Banneker used his knowledge of mechanics to help farmers construct their mills. By 1774 the village of Ellicotts Mills had been founded. Ellicott's decision to grow wheat proved fortunate, for the grain became a key source of food for American troops during the Revolutionary War.

Banneker built a close friendship with son George Ellicott, a mathematician and astronomer. George lent Banneker a number of books on astronomy with the intention of teaching Banneker the various equations. He never got the chance, as Banneker quickly absorbed the information, making note of the errors in calculation he found along the way.

Banneker traveled on horseback to Philadelphia in 1776 to attend the Second Continental Congress, where he watched as statesman and future U.S. President Thomas Jefferson submitted the Declaration of Independence.

It was an inspired Banneker who returned to his farm to

help in the war effort. Following Ellicott's lead, he planted wheat for the soldiers of the Revolutionary Army.

Banneker's life was always wrapped up in the sciences. Sometime after his mother died, he sold his family farm to the Ellicotts so that he could devote full time to his study of nature and the stars. As part of the sale agreement, he kept the house he had grown up in.

Neighbors often commented that Banneker must have been a lazy old man because he slept well into the morning while others were out tending to their farms. What they didn't know was that he spent nearly every night out gazing at the heavens, mapping the paths of the stars and planets, and working on an almanac.

On the basis of his calculations, Banneker correctly predicted that a solar eclipse would take place on April 14, 1789, contradicting the forecasts of prominent mathematicians and astronomers of the day.

BANNEKER AND JEFFERSON

By an act of Congress, a parcel of land along the Maryland-Virginia border was selected as the site for the U.S. capital. In 1789 President George Washington instructed Secretary of State Jefferson to put together a team of surveyors and architects to design the new city.

Major Andrew Ellicott, the son and namesake of Banneker's old friend, was chosen as chief surveyor for the task force, which was headed by L'Enfant, a Frenchman who had served as an engineering officer in the Revolutionary War. Upon Ellicott's advice, Jefferson was prompted to recommend Banneker, making him the nation's first Black presidential appointee.

The move surprised many, historians said, including the editors of the Georgetown *Weekly Ledger*, which had been critical of Jefferson's theories on the genetic inferiority of Africans.

Early on Jefferson, himself a slaveowner with a Black concubine named Sally Hemmings, had said that "the blacks are inferior to the whites in the endowments of both body and mind."

In a March 1791 article describing Banneker's selection, the writer said: "[He is] an Ethiopian, whose ability as a surveyor and an astronomer already prove that Mr. Jefferson's concluding that race of men were void of mental endowment was without foundation."

Historians said that L'Enfant resigned over disputes with bureaucrats who were not pleased with the idea of a French-born architect heading up the design of the U.S. capital. Banneker offered to reproduce the plans from memory and did so within two days.

THE ALMANAC

In 1792 Banneker published his almanac, which offered weather data, tidal information on the Chesapeake Bay, recipes, medical remedies, poems, and abolitionist essays. Also included in the text was information on sunrises and sunsets, festivals and holidays, and phases of the moon. It is the first scientific book written by an African American. The book, which was updated yearly for ten years, was read widely throughout Maryland, Virginia, Delaware, and Pennsylvania.

In 1792 James McHenry, a powerful Maryland legislator who later served as secretary of war in the Washington Cabinet, wrote a letter supporting Banneker's newly completed book. "I consider this Negro as a fresh proof that the powers of mind are disconnected with the color of the skin. . . . In every civilized country, we shall find thousands of whites, liberally educated, and who have enjoyed greater opportunities of instruction than this Negro. Yet many are inferior to him in those intellectual requirements and capacities that form the most characteristic feature of the human race."

As McHenry's letter suggests, Banneker's accomplishments were diminished by the racial attitudes that existed around him. Even his supporters displayed passive acceptance of such thoughts. In the preface to Banneker's 1796 almanac, the editor wrote:

> To whom do you think that you are indebted to for this entertainment? Why, to a Black Man—Strange! Is a Black capable of compiling an almanac? Indeed, it is no less strange than true; and a clever, wise and long-headed Black he is.
>
> The labours of the justly celebrated Banneker will likewise furnish you with a very important lesson, Courteous reader, which you will not find in any other almanac, namely that the Maker of the Universe is no respecter of colours; that the colour of the skin is no way connected with the strength of mind or intellectual powers; that although the God of Nature has marked the face of the African with a darker hue than his brethren, He has given him a soul equally capable of refinement.

Banneker's fame as a self-made astronomer meant nothing. Though he was a free man, he could not vote. He also was well aware of the treatment of fellow Africans who were slaves and spoke out via his almanac and other writings in protest against the injustice and immorality of the slave industry.

Reacting to Jefferson's comments about Blacks, Banneker sent a handwritten copy of his first almanac along with a twelve-page letter:

> We are a race of beings who have long labored under the abuse and censure of the world. We have long been considered rather as brutish than human, and scarcely capable of mental endowments. Sir, I hope ... that you are a man far less inflexible in senti-

ments of this nature than many others. I apprehend that your sentiments are concurrent with mine, which are that our universal Father hath given being to all. . . . How pitiable it is to reflect that, although you were so fully convinced of the benevolence of the Father of mankind that you should at the same time counteract His mercies in detaining by fraud and violence so numerous a part of my brethren under groaning captivity and cruel oppression. When the tyranny of the British crown was exerted to reduce you to servitude, your abhorrence was so excited that you publicly held forth this true and invaluable doctrine. . . . "We hold these truths to be self-evident, that all men are created equal, and that they are endowed by their Creator with certain inalienable rights; that among these are life, liberty, and the pursuit of happiness. . . . " The Almanac is a production of my arduous study. I have long had unbounded desires to become acquainted with the secrets of nature, and I have had to gratify my curiosity herein through my own assiduous application to astronomical study. I need not recount to you the many difficulties and disadvantages I have had to encounter.

Jefferson, apparently swayed by the letter, sent it and a copy of Banneker's almanac to the French Academy of Sciences. Another copy made its way to the British Parliament. In a letter to the secretary of the French academy, Jefferson announced, "We now have in the United States a Negro who is a very respectable mathematician."

In his letter to Banneker, however, despite his positive tone, particularly by the standards of his day, Jefferson still reflected a popular notion among Whites that Africans had to prove themselves on Euro-American terms:

Nobody wishes more than I do to see such proofs as you exhibit that nature has given to our Black brethren talents equal to those of other colors of men, and that the appearance of want of them is owing only to the degraded condition of their existence both in Africa and America. I can add, with truth, that no one wishes more ardently to see a good system commenced for raising the condition both of their body and mind, to what it ought to be, as fast as the imbecility of their present existence, and other circumstances which cannot be neglected, will admit. I [consider your almanac] a document to which your whole color had a right, for their justification against the doubts which have been entertained of them.

POLITICAL IDEALIST

Also in 1792 Banneker, through his almanac, proposed the creation of a "Peace Department" within the executive branch to replace the office of secretary of war. His seven-point plan included the following:

1. Let a Secretary of Peace be appointed to preside in this office.
2. Let a power be given to this Secretary to establish and maintain free schools in every city, village and township of the United States and let him be made responsible for the talents, principles and morals of all his schoolmasters.
3. Let every family in the United States be furnished at public expense, by the Secretary and his office, with a copy of the American edition of the Bible.
4. Let the following sentence be inscribed in letters of gold over the door of every home in the United States: "The Son of Man Came into the World, Not to Destroy Men's Lives But to Save Them."

5. To inspire a veneration for human life and the horror of shedding human blood, let all those laws be repealed which authorize juries, judges, sheriffs, or hangmen to assume the resentments of individuals and to commit murder in cold blood in any case whatever.

6. To subdue a passion for war which education, added to human depravity, has made universal, a familiarity with the instruments of death as well as all military shows should be carefully avoided; military dress and military titles laid aside.

7. Let a large room, adjoining the Federal Hall, be appointed for transacting the business and preserving all the records of this office. Over the door of this room, let there be a sign, on which the figures of a Lamb, a Dove, and an Olive Branch should be painted, together with the following inscription in letters of gold: "Peace on earth—good will to man. Ah! Why will Men forget that they are brethren?"

Banneker stopped publishing the almanac in 1802 because he was too old and sickly to continue. He spent his final years back on the Maryland farm, playing host to the distinguished scientists and artists of his day. He died on October 25, 1806, and was buried near the cabin which had served as his lifelong home.

A MOVE TO CREATE A MONUMENT

In 1991 a committee of prominent Black Washington, D.C., residents began pressing the city to place a statue of the mathematician-astronomer among the city's many monuments to Whites. If approved, the statue would be only the second of an African American on public ground in the nation's capital (a statue honoring educator Mary McLeod Bethune was dedicated in 1974 and sits in Lincoln Park on Capitol Hill).

For different reasons, several dozen luminaries from the

city's academic and international communities also want to erect an outdoor monument to L'Enfant. Both men are honored in Washington in other ways, L'Enfant with a large plaza off Constitution Avenue in Southeast Washington, and Banneker with a high school named for him and a small traffic circle within L'Enfant Plaza.

James Forten, 1766–1842

James Forten, Sr., invented and perfected the modern design for a ship's sail.

Forten lived during an era of American adventure on the high seas, particularly for Blacks. In 1776 at least one fifth of the merchant seamen in Philadelphia were free Africans. By 1846 there were roughly six thousand Black seamen, according to the *National Anti-Slavery Standard*.

BLACKS AND THE HIGH SEAS

The coastal cities of New York, Boston, and New Bedford and Nantucket Island all had employed large numbers of Blacks. During the 1830s, for example, the Black population of Nantucket jumped from 270 to more than 570. Similarly, New Bedford's African population soared from 385 to nearly 800.

John Mashow, a free Black, was among those who migrated north. He traveled up from the rural South as a boy in search of work. He eventually established his own shipbuilding company in 1831 and was the builder of the *Jireh Swift*, a whaler that was sunk by the Confederate battleship *Shenandoah* during the Civil War. Whaling ships, such as the *Loper*, sported nearly all-Black crews, led by a Black captain. *Loper* Captain Absalom F. Boston was the grandson of Prince Boston, an enslaved African, and was the first Black seaman to be paid for his work. The elder Boston had been hired out by his owner, who in turn was paid. But a Massachusetts court ruled that the wages should go directly to the man who had earned them. In 1837 another ship, the *Rising States*, was manned entirely by Blacks.

James Forten was born free in Philadelphia in 1766. His parents, Sarah and Thomas Forten, were also born free. Forten's great-grandfather had been brought to America from his native West Africa during the 1660s. He eventually earned enough to purchase his freedom.

Thomas, Forten's father, was a Philadelphia sailmaker, who fitted out small vessels. The elder Forten passed along his expertise to his son. Thomas died in a boating accident in 1775, two years after enrolling James in the Africa School, run by noted Quaker abolitionist Anthony Benezet. After his father's death, Forten worked briefly in a grocery store to help support his mother. The elder Forten died broke, leaving James no choice but to quit school.

Robert Bridges, a White sailmaker, eventually hired James. It began a long relationship between the two. At fourteen Forten signed on as a powder boy with the Revolutionary War ship *Royal Louis*. He was on a crew that included twenty Blacks. He was captured by the British and held aboard the notorious prison ship *Jersey*. Sea Captain Daniel Brewton was a prisoner on the British ship with Forten. The two were released during a general prisoner exchange and came out of the ordeal lasting friends.

After the war Forten enlisted as a merchant seaman and went to England. A year later he returned to Philadelphia, where he apprenticed with Bridges. Bridges promoted Forten to foreman of the sail loft in 1786. When Bridges retired in 1798, he lent Forten the money to buy the business. At thirty-two years of age, Forten commanded a thirty-eight-man crew—half Black, half White.

Forten's reputation as a sailmaker grew along with his wealth. A Black rights advocate, he served as an officer of the African Masonic Lodge and was a member of the St. Thomas African Episcopal Church.

ABOLITIONIST

Forten's contributions also came outside the inventor's world. A staunch abolitionist, Forten was an outspoken advocate of equal rights and led reform movements before the emergence of the famed abolitionist Frederick Douglass. Forten spent much of the three-hundred-thousand-dollar fortune he eventually accumulated financing liberation causes. With his money, Forten bought freedom for a number of enslaved Africans. Among Forten's contemporaries were Black leaders Richard Allen and Absalom Jones. Forten's home also served as a stop along the Underground Railroad.

Forten, Jones, and Allen were among those who recruited more than twenty-five hundred free Blacks to battle the British in the War of 1812. Forten also donated money to William Lloyd Garrison, founder and publisher of *The Liberator.*

Charlotte Vandine, Forten's second wife, was born free in Pennsylvania. She was not yet twenty-one when she and thirty-nine-year-old Forten married in 1805. Forten's first wife had died eighteen months earlier. Their marriage was a brief one.

Margaretta, Forten's eldest daughter, was born in Philadelphia in 1808. Margaretta distinguished herself as an abolitionist and educator until her death in 1875. Forten's other children were Harriet, Sarah, Mary, James junior, Robert, Thomas, and William.

By the time Margaretta was born, her father had moved from Southwark—a seedy part of Philadelphia with wharves and warehouses, disease and epidemics—to a three-story brick house at 92 Lombard Street, located in a well-to-do Black neighborhood. Bridges lent Forten the money to buy that house as well as homes for Forten's mother and his sister's family.

41

LOMBARD STREET

The house on Lombard was bustling with activity. With the family, hired help, apprentices, and journeymen counted in, there were as many as fifteen people living in the house in 1810, according to federal census figures. Ten years later that number had grown to eighteen; and by 1830 there were twenty-two residents.

Among the visitors to the Forten home was a leader of the American Colonization Society. The two were engulfed in a discussion on Haitian politics when, to make a point, Forten, who was fluent in both English and French, produced a letter he had received from his brother-in-law Charles in Port-au-Prince. The guest, who was White, could not read the letter, written in French, and apparently was embarrassed as Forten's daughter Margaretta read it to him. Forten recalled in a letter that his guest left the house to attend a meeting to discuss the intellectual inferiority of Blacks.

A BLACK SCHOOL

Despite Forten's success, Blacks were closed out of the education system their taxes supported. He and Charlotte taught their children themselves. Other parents either did the same or relied on churches or charities.

The Fortens eventually established a school for Blacks, owned by Blacks, with Grace Bustill Douglass, the daughter of Black community leader Cyrus Bustill. Grace's husband, Robert Douglass, was a barber from the West Indies. They hired Britton E. Chamberlain as the school's first teacher.

James Forten died in 1842.

Norbert Rillieux, 1806–1894

Norbert Rillieux's development of a sugar-refining process revolutionized the sugar industry. The lack of recognition he received, however, troubled him his whole life long.

Early Innovators

In 1843 Rillieux developed a method for refining sugar. It consisted of a series of vacuum pans combined in a step-by-step process to make heated evaporated sugar into crystallized granules.

THE SUGAR INDUSTRY

Prior to Rillieux's invention, sugar was an expensive luxury, used only on special occasions. The old process used to make sugar—known as the Jamaica Train—was a slow, dangerous, and costly exercise, usually performed by slaves. They worked over open, boiling kettles, ladling sugarcane juice from one container to another. A large number of workers were scalded to death by the boiling substance, while many more received severe burns.

The end product of this dangerous process was a dark, thick syrupy substance, looking more like caramel than the granulated form known today. The syrupy sugar was poured into cones to dry and was bought and sold in this condition.

Sugarcane and sugar beet are the two major sources of sugar, which has served as a major crop for a number of nations. The sugar beet, which is 20 percent sucrose, provides about one third of the world's sugar supply. Cuba and India, both cane harvesters, supply about one third of the world's cane sugar.

The concept for Rillieux's partial vacuum pan invention was simple: to bring liquid sugar to a boil and allow it to evaporate without letting it get too hot. If sugar gets too hot, it will not turn to the crystal form we have become used to. Rather, it takes on a caramel-like quality. Rillieux's evaporation process is a multiple-effect operation in which a series of vacuum pans heat one another in sequence, thus controlling the overall temperature and producing the desired crystallized form.

The significance of Rillieux's process to the American sugar-making industry cannot be overstated. At the time the method was introduced, American sugarcane planters lagged far behind Brazil and Haiti, which were still using cheap slave labor, making their sugar production much cheaper. Rillieux made it possible for the United States to dominate the market. The basic concept of his evaporation process is still used for things like freeze-drying food, pigments, and other industrial products.

FREEBORN

Rillieux, a quadroon, was born in New Orleans on March 17, 1806, to Vincent Rillieux, a wealthy engineer, and Constance Vivant, a slave on his plantation. The elder Rillieux was an inventor in his own right. He was credited with the invention of a steam-operated bailing press. Despite his mother's status, Norbert was regarded as free.

A lack of educational opportunities for Blacks in this country forced Rillieux to send Norbert to Paris for his schooling.

TRIAL AND ERROR

At L'École Centrale, Rillieux found his niche in the study of engineering, and at twenty-four he became an instructor of applied mechanics at the French school. In 1830 his series of papers on steam engines and practical applications drew a positive response from the scientific community. During this period he also began developing his multiple-effect evaporation theory—the cornerstone of his invention.

Prior to Rillieux's breakthrough, other scientists had made vacuum pans and condensing coils—to remove the steam—for refining sugarcane juice, but they were not very effective. Rillieux's process also was not immediately successful. His first attempt at making an evaporation device in 1834 was a failure. He failed again in 1841.

The early setbacks caused Rillieux to doubt his concept until a New Orleans plantation owner convinced him to try again. By 1843 he had finally managed to produce a workable process, for which he obtained a patent. He secured a second patent in 1846 for improvements to the original.

In his 1843 patent application, he said, "[T]he first improvement is in the manner of connecting a steam engine with the evaporating pan . . . in such a manner that . . . the flow of steam be so regulated by a weighted or other valve. . . . "

In his second patent application, he described the process in more detail:

1. The method of heating the saccharine juice in a heater preparatory to its introduction in the evaporating pans, by means of the waste hot water or escape steam from the evaporating pans.

2. The method of clarifying saccharine juice by heating it in a heater provided with a spout for the discharge of the impurities in the form of scum, and a pipe for drawing off the clear liquid.

3. The method of cooling and partially evaporating saccharine juice or other liquids by discharging the same in the form of spray or drops in a chamber, where it meets with the current of air; . . . and this I also claim in combination with a condenser whereby the liquid intended to be concentrated is prepared for the evaporating pans and used as a means of condensing the vapor from the pans in which it is to be concentrated or by means of which the water used for the condensing jet is re-cooled.

4. The method, substantially as described, of combining a vacuum striking pan with a series of evaporating pans, the last of which is independent of the striking pan, and the last of the series of evaporating pans can be in connection with the condenser and work independently of each other.

As a result of his invention, Rillieux, who was in Paris, was offered the post of chief engineer in Edmund Forstall's sugar factory in New Orleans. He refused the position upon learning of a disagreement between Forstall and his father.

REVOLUTIONIZING AN INDUSTRY

Rillieux's machine was first installed at the Myrtle Grove plantation in Louisiana in 1845 and soon appeared throughout Louisiana, Cuba, and Mexico. Today the process is still used in the making of sugar as well as soap, gelatin, condensed milk, and glue, in the recovery of waste liquors in distilleries, and at paper factories. In addition, the process is utilized in the recovery of waste liquids in factories and distilleries.

Rillieux also was credited with a number of engineering devices still in use, such as a lunette, or sight glass, which allows the monitoring of the refining process; a catchall, used to keep sugar droplets from spreading through vapor; and cast-iron containers, replacing more expensive copper kettles, thought in his day to be essential to the sugar-making process.

But while his invention made the United States a sugar giant, Rillieux was never recognized for his efforts. None of the chemistry, physics, or technical journals of his time mentioned his work. He continued to be excluded from social life in the New Orleans area despite his accomplishments. The Civil War was drawing near, and there were restrictions on the movements of Blacks throughout the South. A Black person, in general, could not walk the streets freely without carrying a pass from the government—a precursor to what followed nearly a century and an ocean away in South Africa.

Rillieux ran into more bigotry after he had developed an engineering plan to attack the mosquitoes that spread yellow fever and lived in the New Orleans sewer system. The infestation had reached crisis proportions, resulting in numerous deaths. His plan called for the draining of swampy areas in and around the city, which served as breeding grounds for the insects. But his plan was refused by city officials, many of them publicly stating that they would not accept as valid the work of a Black man. Years later his sewer plan, developed and reintroduced by Whites, was implemented in New Orleans.

BACK TO EUROPE

Frustrated with the city's racial attitudes, Rillieux eventually left New Orleans. More restrictions against free Blacks in the South sent him back in 1854 to France, where he became an Egyptologist. He returned to Paris and was named headmaster of L'École Centrale.

In Europe the engineer also turned his attention to using his sugar-refining process with the sugar beet, used widely throughout France. He patented the process in 1881. He lived in Paris until his death on October 8, 1894. He was buried in Père Lachaise Cemetery.

According to the inscription on Rillieux's grave, there was a Mrs. Rillieux, Emily Cuckow, some twenty years his junior. Little is known of her except that she died eighteen years after her husband.

After the turn of the century, the fame that had escaped Rillieux during his lifetime began to develop. In 1903 J. G. McIntosh, in his book *Technology of Sugar*, wrote that the engineer "may, therefore, with all justice, be regarded as one of the greatest benefactors of the sugar industry."

In the 1920s a movement of scholars in Holland to honor Rillieux spread throughout the world. In 1934, after a struggle, admirers of Rillieux succeeded in convincing the city of New Orleans to honor him with a plaque, designed in Amsterdam, which now rests in the Louisiana State Museum.

Andrew Jackson Beard, 1850–1910

Prior to Andrew Jackson Beard's invention, railroad car coupling was a dangerous job. It required that a railroad worker

47

brace himself between two railway cars and drop a metal spike into a slot once the cars were close enough together. Almost daily it seemed that men were losing fingers, hands, even arms during the maneuver. Many more were crushed to death.

Beard, a former slave, invented the automatic railroad coupler, also known as the Jenny Coupler. It allowed trains to be joined together without human assistance. Beard's coupler was patented on November 23, 1897. He later sold the invention to a New York firm for fifty thousand dollars, a tremendous sum. An improved model, the forerunner to the modern-day version, was approved in 1899.

Beard was born in 1849 in Jefferson County, Alabama. Freed when he was fourteen years old, he married a year later. Beard was a farmer by trade. For five years he operated a farm near Birmingham, Alabama, until the trips into Montgomery with fifty bushels of apples became too much for him to bear.

In 1872 he turned his attention elsewhere, building and operating a flour mill in Hardwicks, Alabama. Eventually he began work on the creation of his own version of a plow, patenting and selling the concept in 1884 for four thousand dollars. He built a second plow in 1887 and sold it for fifty-two hundred dollars. With the money Beard started a real estate business from which he earned a profit of about thirty thousand dollars. In 1889 he invented a rotary steam engine that was less expensive to build and run and was less likely to explode than other steam engines. It was patented on July 5, 1892.

Not much is known of Beard's life after 1897.

Jan Earnst Matzeliger, 1852–1889

Jan Earnst Matzeliger designed and patented a "shoe-lasting" machine, which automatically stitched the shoe leather to the sole of the shoe. The invention reduced the cost of making shoes. It also put the United States squarely at the center of the shoemaking map.

The last is a wooden model of the human foot around which a shoe is constructed. Prior to Matzeliger's invention, shoe lasting was a costly and painstaking process, requiring highly skilled craftspeople. When it was determined that the upper leather had properly been drawn over the last, it was tacked to the inner sole. The excess leather at the toe was cut and drawn into plaits, which were shaved off, leaving a smooth appearance. Matzeliger's machine made these tasks easier.

Matzeliger was born on September 15, 1852, in Paramaribo, in the Dutch colony of Surinam (also known as Dutch Guiana). His mother was a Black native of the country, and his father was an engineer from a wealthy family in Holland who had been sent to Surinam to oversee a machine works.

At age ten Matzeliger worked as an apprentice cobbler in a government-run machine shop. There he showed an interest in and an aptitude for mechanics. He had little, if any, formal education.

COMING TO AMERICA

At nineteen, not certain of what he would do, but certain that he would not find it at home, Matzeliger signed onto an East Indian merchant ship. He spent the next two years as a seaman. He left the ship in Philadelphia, where he worked a number of odd jobs, including a brief stint with a cobbler. He could barely speak English and knew no one. His early years in America were fraught with loneliness.

In 1876 the slender Matzeliger moved north to Lynn, Massachusetts, where he lived the remainder of his life. At the time Lynn, a town of about thirty-five thousand people, was regarded as the nation's major shoe-manufacturing center, producing more than half the country's shoes. Matzeliger parlayed his knowledge of mechanics to secure a job with the Harney Brothers company, a local shoemaking factory. As he moved from job to job, Matzeliger became more familiar with the shoe-making business and its various machines.

At the same time Matzeliger worked on improving his English-speaking and -writing skills, buying physics books with the little money he made.

ODDS AND ENDS

Matzeliger apparently was frustrated by the amount of time required to last shoes by hand and decided to work on his own time at nights on a machine to speed up the process. He rented a room over the Old West Lynn Mission and began work on a prototype machine, using wood scraps, old cigar boxes, and bits of discarded hardware. He also employed a forge that had been abandoned by a local Blacksmith to mold the gears and inner workings. By 1880, after five years of tinkering, he had assembled a machine for plaiting leather at the toe of a shoe.

While dozens of shoemaking machines were in use prior to Matzeliger's invention, none of them possessed the ability to attach the upper portion of the shoe to the sole. In 1790 the London cabinetmaker Thomas Saint had designed the first sewing machine specifically designed for making shoes. Frenchman Marc Brunel followed suit some twenty years later, inventing a machine in London that could mass-produce nailed combat boots. By 1841 Thomas Archibald, an English machinist, was the first to apply the concept of a needle to the process of attaching the uppers to the sole. But according to the common wisdom of the day, the process of lasting shoes by machine was just plain impossible.

In 1883 Matzeliger's application for a patent was refused because it was too complex to understand. The Patent Office sent a representative to see the device firsthand. It was finally accepted in 1886.

LYNN: SHOEMAKING CAPITAL

Matzeliger's machine made Lynn the undisputed capital of the shoe-making world. During the next two years he successfully applied for four more patents for improvements to his original machine.

Matzeliger originally had rejected offers as high as fifteen hundred dollars to buy his invention and eventually secured backing from Charles H. Delnow and Melville S. Nichols to mass-produce the machine through Matzeliger's Union Lasting Shoe Company. He also owned a large block of stock in the company.

To make ends meet, he worked as a cobbler, attended night school, and taught oil painting. Unable to continue financing production of his machine, he sold the patent in 1890 to Sidney Winslow and George W. Brown in exchange for stock. (By 1897, eight years after Matzeliger's death, Winslow had pulled together several lasting machine factories to form the New York Machine Company. Two years later he formed the multimillion-dollar United Shoe Machinery Corporation. Over the next twelve years the corporation cornered more than 98 percent of the nation's shoe market. By 1955 the corporation had grown into a multibillion-dollar industry.)

Matzeliger never profited from his invention. He was out of the shoemaking picture, and his contribution all but forgotten, save for the unusual nickname bestowed on his creation. It became known as the "Nigger-Head" machine.

MATZELIGER'S LEGACY

Matzeliger lived out the remainder of his short life in relative poverty and obscurity. He developed tuberculosis in 1886 and died in August 1889, apparently unaware of the effect his machine had on the shoemaking industry. He was thirty-seven.

Shortly before his death, Matzeliger was allowed to join the White North Church in Lynn, although not as an official member. He was, however, allowed to attend services and even taught Sunday school. The local Catholic, Episcopal, and Unitarian churches in Lynn apparently saw Matzeliger's Blackness as not worthy of their god's love. It was a slight he never forgot.

Some years after his death Matzeliger was remembered by the Lynn church when it was discovered that his gift of his entire holdings in his Union Lasting Shoe Company and one third of his interest in another company had increased in value. He had bequeathed the stocks to the church with express directions that they not be used to aid anyone associated with the religions that had snubbed him.

North Church discovered the value of Matzeliger's gift at the most opportune time. The church was heavily in debt and used the money from the sale of the stock—more than ten thousand dollars—to retire the debt. Soon a life-size statue of Matzeliger was erected inside the church. During the ceremony a White church woman read a eulogy, while the Reverend A. J. Covell read a sermon dedicated to the inventor's memory.

Matzeliger was honored with a statue by the city of Lynn and the local National Association for the Advancement of Colored People (NAACP) in May 1967. The U.S. Postal Service issued a postage stamp honoring Matzeliger and held a special ceremony in Lynn in 1991. He was the fourteenth African American to be featured on a stamp honoring the nation's Black heritage. The stamp, designed by Barbara Higgins Bond of Teaneck, New Jersey, depicts a likeness of Matzeliger superimposed on a line drawing of his machine.

Today shoemaking machines still are based on his early invention.

Louis Temple, 1800–1854

Louis Temple was not a whaling man, but in 1845 he introduced the harpoon that changed the whaling industry. His

Early Innovators

Temple's Toggle or Temple's Iron was the standard harpoon used during the second half of the nineteenth century.

The harpoon in use prior to his invention was a simple barb attached to a rope. The short spear allowed a seaman to approach a whale for a close-in kill, but the barb was not reliable and often fell out of the harpooned creature. The barbs on Temple's harpoon pivoted and actually locked into a whale's skin, making the huge mammals easier to subdue. His invention more than doubled the yearly catch.

Temple's harpoon was in reality a throwback to a weapon used by prehistoric whale hunters. It is doubtful that Temple or his contemporaries were aware of that forerunner.

NORTHWARD

Temple was born a slave in Richmond, Virginia, in 1800. Freed in 1829, and with no formal education, he moved north to New Bedford, Massachusetts. There he found work as a metalsmith. The same year he married Mary Clark, and they had three children. By 1836 when Temple set up shop on Coppin's Wharf, a whaling area, he was one of 315,000 free Blacks in the United States. By 1845 he had moved to Walnut Street.

Whaling was a major industry throughout New England, providing thousands of jobs for seamen, many of whom were African. Temple learned from his customers that the barb-headed harpoons being used to catch whales were not effective because they allowed them to escape. Temple never patented his harpoon, leaving others free to sell it as their own.

In 1854 Temple began construction on a new site for his shop. It was never completed. Temple was injured after falling into a hole near his planned shop on School Street and was unable to return to work. The hole had been left by a construction crew working on a sewer line. He petitioned the city for reparations, and on March 28, 1854, he was awarded two thousand dollars. It was never paid to Temple or his heirs.

53

He died in May, leaving an estate of fifteen hundred dollars. When his estate was settled, most of his holdings were used to pay his debts.

Lewis Howard Latimer, 1848–1928

Lewis Howard Latimer, a pioneer in the development of the electric light bulb, was the only Black member of Thomas A. Edison's research team of noted scientists. While Edison invented the incandescent bulb, it was Latimer, a member of the Edison Pioneers, and a former assistant to telephone inventor Alexander Graham Bell, who developed and patented the process for manufacturing carbon filaments.

Latimer was born in Chelsea, Massachusetts, on September 4, 1848, and reared in Boston with three brothers and sisters. His father, George Latimer, a former slave, had fled to Boston from Virginia during the 1830s. By October 1842 the elder Latimer's whereabouts had become known to James B. Gray, his former owner. When Gray came to Boston that year to lay claim to his "property," he was met with opposition. Abolitionists Frederick Douglass and William Lloyd Garrison took up Latimer's banner, eventually raising the four hundred dollars needed to gain him his freedom from Gray. Soon thereafter the state of Massachusetts passed a law, the Personal Liberty Law, that prohibited state officials from taking part in the fugitive slave hunts.

As a young boy Latimer sold copies of Garrison's newspaper, *The Liberator,* on the streets of Boston, but childhood ended when he was ten, and his father deserted his wife, leaving her to bring up their four children alone.

At sixteen Latimer joined the Union navy as a cabin boy on the USS *Massasoit.* After his honorable discharge in 1865 Latimer returned to Boston. Skills he had developed in mechanical drawing landed him a position with Crosby and Gould, patent solicitors.

Early Innovators

Latimer's drafting skills were self-taught, coming from a set of drafting books he purchased with the little money he made and from the tutoring of professional draftsmen. He also had purchased a set of drafting tools with which to practice. When he asked his employers if he could submit a few drawings, the request was reluctantly approved. His work, however, impressed them to the extent that they promoted him to junior draftsman. He later advanced to chief draftsman. He stayed with the company eleven years.

During this time Latimer met Mary Wilson. The couple were married on December 10, 1873. To mark the ceremony, he wrote a poem to his wife:

Let others boast of maidens fair,
Of eyes of blue and golden hair;
My heart like needles ever true
Turns to the maid of ebon hue.
I love her form of matchless grace,
The dark brown beauty of her face,
Her lips that speak of love's delight,
Her eyes that gleam as stars at night.
O'er marble Venus let them rage,
Who set the fashions of the age;
Each to his taste, but as for me,
My Venus shall be ebony.

They had two daughters.

Stimulated no doubt by the creativity all around him in an office where invention patents were handled, Latimer sought to make his own creations. His first patent, approved on February 10, 1874, was for a "water closet for railway cars." The invention added a closed, pivoted bottom to the normally open-ended water closet. The bottom closed or opened automatically by raising or lowering the seat cover.

55

The office where Latimer worked was located near a school for hearing-disabled children run by Alexander Graham Bell, whose invention of the telephone came while he was trying to develop a device that would help the young people at his school hear. During the 1870s Bell hired Crosby and Gould to prepare the blueprints for his telephone. At Bell's insistence, Latimer was chosen as the draftsman for the patent, which was approved in 1876.

Three years later Thomas A. Edison invented the incandescent electric light, which revolutionized technology worldwide. Latimer also was involved in experiments and studies of electricity and eventually made improvements to the Edison original.

Latimer left Crosby and Gould in 1880 to work as a draftsman for Hiram Maxim, the inventor of the machine gun and head of the United States Electric Lighting Company in Bridgeport, Connecticut.

In 1881 Latimer and fellow inventor Joseph V. Nichols received a patent for their invention of the first incandescent light bulb with a carbon filament. Prior to this breakthrough, filaments had been made from paper.

Latimer assigned his patent to the U.S. Electric Lighting Company, which had relocated to New York. Later that year another Latimer patent was assigned to U.S. Electric. His globe supporter allowed carbons to be connected to the globe, or bulb, by means of end clasps between the carbons and the bulb. These early wooden sockets are on display at Washington, D.C.'s Smithsonian Institution.

Other Latimer inventions included "an apparatus for cooling and disinfecting" (patented on January 12, 1886); locking racks for hat and coats and umbrellas (March 24, 1886); and "book supports" (February 7, 1905).

Latimer supervised the installation of Hiram Maxim's electric lights in New York, Philadelphia, Montreal, and London during the early 1880s. In 1881 he was sent to London to set up that city's streetlighting for the Maxim-Weston Electric Light Company. He ran into a few difficulties dealing with British businessmen, who apparently were forced to get used to taking orders from a man of color. "I was in hot water," he wrote in his journal. The London trip also turned into something of a delayed honeymoon for Latimer and wife, Mary, as the two toured the fabled city.

Latimer, who had achieved fame as one of the foremost experts on electric lighting, went to work for Brooklyn's Olmstead Electric Lighting Company once he returned from Great Britain. Later he accepted a post with the Acme Electric Light Company in New York.

In 1884 Latimer joined the engineering department of the Edison Electric Light Company. In 1890 he transferred to the legal department, where he served as an expert court witness in million-dollar cases involving Edison's patents. More often than not, Latimer's testimony proved to make the difference between winning and losing.

Also in 1890, his book *Incandescent Electric Lighting* was published. It was the first known book on the subject of lighting.

Around the same time the Edison company was renamed the General Electric Company. In 1896 GE joined forces with another electric giant, Westinghouse, in the Board of Patent Control. The board, which was set up to protect their patents against encroachments, hired Latimer as its chief draftsman and expert witness, positions he held until 1911.

Along the way Latimer had met Edwin W. Hammer, a New York engineer, who had once been an assistant in the old Edison labs and had started a collection of the inventor's incandescent lamps. The Latimer lamp is included in the Hammer Collection of more than eight hundred items on display in Detroit.

Throughout his life Latimer worked on behalf of civil rights groups, speaking out against racism. He also taught mechanical drawing to students at a New York City community center. An illness he contracted in 1924 led to his death on December 11, 1928, at his home in Flushing, New York.

The Edison Pioneers was a group comprised of Edison's colleagues in electrical research. Latimer was the only person of African ancestry in the organization when it formed on January 24, 1918. The group's tribute to Latimer at the time of his death reads: "We hardly mourn his inevitable going so much as we rejoice in pleasant memory at having been associated with him in a great work for all people under a great man. Broadmindedness, versatility in the accomplishment of things intellectual and cultural, a linguist, a devoted husband and father, all were characteristic of him, and his genial presence will be missed from our gatherings."

In 1929, on the fiftieth anniversary of Edison's invention of the electric light, Latimer's two daughters were the guests of honor of the Edison Pioneers' annual meeting. By the time the seventy-fifth anniversary was noted in 1954, no mention of Latimer was made.

A New York City public school was dedicated in Latimer's name on May 10, 1968, in Brooklyn. Tributes were paid to Latimer by the members of the New York Legislature, the Borough of Brooklyn, and the New York City Board of Education. Latimer's grandson, Gerald Norman, presented a portrait of him to the school. Latimer's granddaughter, Winifred Latimer Norman, also was in attendance.

Granville T. Woods, 1856–1910

Granville T. Woods was awarded more than 35 patents for his electrical inventions and more than 150 total patents. Known as the Black Edison, Woods was one of the pioneers of the Industrial Revolution.

Woods was born in Columbus, Ohio, on April 23, 1856.

Early Innovators

Thanks to the 1787 Northwest Ordinance, which disallowed slavery in the territory that became Ohio, he was born free. However, Ohio was the first nonslave state to invoke the Black Laws, which effectively prohibited the movement of Blacks in the state through curfews and hiring practices.

Woods started elementary school, but by ten he had to find a job. He found work in a machine shop.

At sixteen Woods traveled west to Missouri and got a job as a fireman-engineer with the Iron Mountain Railroad. He became interested in learning about electricity, a rapidly growing field. He pored through every book he could find on electricity from the library and from friends and employers. In 1874 he went to Springfield, Illinois, where he worked in a rolling mill. Two years later he reached the East Coast to study electrical and mechanical engineering. In 1878 he signed on as an engineer on the *Ironsides*, a British steamer. He worked for two years on the ship and visited nearly every country on the globe. Two years later he landed a similar job with the Danville & Southern Railroad.

By 1881 he had earned enough money to open the Woods Electric Company of Cincinnati, which made telephone, telegraph, and electrical equipment. He also began to study thermal power and steam-driven engines. In 1884 Woods received a patent for his creation of a steam boiler furnace.

That same year he invented a telephone transmitter that could carry a voice over long distance with greater clarity and improved sound. By creating and making use of an alternating current, controlled by the motion of vibrating metal disks, or diaphragms, he invented a transmitter with more range than that which had been available.

In 1885 Woods patented the telegraphony, a device that allowed telegraph stations to send messages via Morse code and orally over the same line. With this device an operator who could read or write Morse code signals could switch the battery off of the main-line Morse code circuit onto a local telephone circuit. This allowed the operator to hear a transmission by putting his or her ear near the telegraph key. The receiving operator could hear the incoming message as audible speech. Woods sold the invention to the American Bell Telephone Company in Boston.

The year 1887 was a busy one for Woods. He created a synchronous multiplex railway telegraph, which allowed messages to be sent to and from moving trains. The device conducted messages via static electricity to the telegraph wires running alongside the tracks without interfering with normal telegraphic communications. With this invention, train conductors and engineers could be apprised of hazards on the tracks ahead. The creation soon became a staple product for Woods's company. His invention became so popular that he devoted his time solely to creating others.

In 1890 Woods moved to New York City, where he and his brother Lyates worked on ideas. Lyates had created a number of his own products and enjoyed his share of commercial success. Also in 1890, Woods invented an electrically heated egg incubator. The device could handle as many as fifty thousand eggs at one time.

A love of the theater prompted the creation of his next invention. He noticed that the dimming system for theater houselights was inconsistent and wasted a great deal of energy. Additionally, electrical fires often resulted when the crude resistor, which also powered an elevator or other energy-eating machines, got too hot. In 1896 Woods designed a new dimming system that was both safe and energy-efficient. The device controlled the strength of an electrical current coming through the generator to the machine to be protected. At the time it was estimated that his device reduced energy consumption by about 40 percent.

In 1898 Woods set up an overhead conducting system for the railroad, replacing expensive and inefficient steam-driven engines with clean, efficient electric trains. The system is in use today with streetcars and trolleys. The new trains became so popular that smoke-spewing steam trains were banned from many cities as pollution hazards.

Another Woods invention was the third rail, which still exists on many city subway tracks. A series of electrical conductors run parallel to the train's path. Each train car carries a collector that connects with the conductors, thus powering the train. Electromagnetic switches control the flow of energy to the conductors from the electrical source. Woods sold the invention to the New York-based General Electric Company in 1901.

General Electric held a number of Woods's patents, as did the Westinghouse Air Brake Company of Pennsylvania, the American Bell Telephone Company of Boston, and the American Engineering Company. Westinghouse, for example, purchased Woods's three patents that led to the invention of the automatic air brake for trains in 1905.

During his life Woods had at least two run-ins with famed inventor Thomas A. Edison. The two met as adversaries in court over who owned the rights to certain electrical inventions. Woods won both verdicts, prompting Edison to offer him a job. Woods refused.

Woods died in New York on January 30, 1910.

Elijah McCoy, 1843–1929

Elijah McCoy was the inventor of a device that allowed machines to be lubricated while they were still in operation. Machinery buyers insisted on McCoy lubrication systems when buying new machines and would take nothing less than what became known as the real McCoy. The inventor's automatic oiling devices became so universal that no heavy-duty machinery was considered adequate without it, and the expression became part of American culture (although some argue it has other origins).

Elijah McCoy was born in Colchester, Ontario, Canada, in 1843 to George and Mildred McCoy. His parents were escaped slaves, who had fled from Kentucky and made it to Canada, riding the Underground Railroad.

When McCoy was a child, his family returned across the border, settling near Ypsilanti, Michigan, where his father worked in the logging industry. For a time he attended grammar school. His parents saved enough money to send their fifteen-year-old son to Edinburgh, Scotland, to serve an apprenticeship in mechanical engineering.

He returned to the United States as a full-fledged engineer. He also returned to a country that placed no value on the credentials of a Black man, no matter how impressive. It was a theme that repeated itself throughout McCoy's life.

WORKING ON THE RAILROAD

McCoy eventually settled for a job as a fireman for the Michigan Central Railroad, his engineering skills going to waste as he shoveled coal. He also was charged with oiling the trains' moving parts. In those days it was common practice to shut down the trains or machines periodically, while the oilmen went around making certain that all moving parts were well greased.

During this period he began to work on self-lubrication devices. In a makeshift workshop he tried to design something that could keep a machine oiled as it operated, eliminating the need for downtime. His plan was to create canals and chambers within the workings of a machine to carry the oil to needed areas. He called his invention the lubricator cup.

By 1872 McCoy had acquired his first patent. With the lubricator cup, patented on July 2, small amounts of oil dripped onto moving engine parts, saving businesses time and money. The device was used with steam engines. A hollow tube projected down from the bottom of the cup into a steam chamber.

There was a valve at the top end of the tube and a piston at the lower end. Steam in the cylinder activated the piston, releasing oil.

A year later McCoy improved on his original model so that oil was released only when there was no longer steam in the chamber. Over the next few years he continued to make and patent modifications to his original design. Soon orders rolled in from factories around the country.

THE REAL MCCOY

By the 1880s McCoy's lubricator cup was the cornerstone product of the McCoy Manufacturing Company in Detroit. But McCoy's success did not save him from the craziness of racism. Often he was asked to speak, appear, or consult to some large company, only to have the invitation rescinded when it was discovered that he was Black. Some companies even canceled their orders for his lubricator despite the fact that they really needed it.

By 1892 he had turned his attention to solving lubrication problems in locomotives, inventing an assortment of lubricating devices. He solved a long-standing problem of how to maintain stable steam pressure within the engine, setting up independent steam and overflow pipes that regulated pressure going in and out of the engine. The system was utilized by western railroads and steamer ships on the Great Lakes.

By 1920 McCoy had applied his lubrication technology to vehicles using air brakes. This invention used a mixture of oil and graphite, a solid lubricant derived from carbon. Eventually McCoy patented more than fifty different lubricating devices. Only two of his patents—an ironing table and a lawn sprinkler—were in areas other than automatic machine lubrication.

Elijah McCoy died in Detroit in 1929 at the age of eighty-five.

Daniel Hale Williams, 1856–1931

The first doctor in the world to perform a successful open-heart operation was Daniel Hale Williams. On July 9, 1893, James Cornish was rushed to Chicago's Provident Hospital with a stab wound to the chest. He had been injured in a fight. He was brought into a small room—too small for the six-person staff in attendance. No transfusion available. No such thing as a heart-lung machine. No electrocardiograph. No anesthetic. And there was no X ray to tell whether the bleeding, which had stopped on the surface, had also stopped inside the body.

Williams opened the chest, found and emptied the blood from the pericardial sac, and sutured it, working less than an inch from Cornish's heart. On August 2 Williams again operated, opening the man's chest to remove excess fluid from the chest cavity.

On August 30 Cornish walked out of Provident Hospital to live for another twenty years. Williams recalled seeing Cornish hard at work one day in the Chicago stockyards.

EARLY YEARS

Williams was born in Holidaysburg, Pennsylvania, in 1856. When he was eleven, his father, a well-to-do barber, died. His mother, unable to care for seven children on her own, sent some to live with family and others to convent school. Young Daniel was apprenticed to a family friend in Baltimore, who was a cobbler.

When he was seventeen, Williams wandered the country. Eventually he went to live with an older sister in Wisconsin, where he met Charles Anderson, a well-known Black barber in Janesville. Williams later said that Anderson became a second father to him. While in high school, Williams worked part-time in Anderson's shop. Many historians say it was here that Williams began to develop the manual dexterity that served him well throughout his life.

Williams eventually went to work for two years as an apprentice with a Dr. Palmer. He then attended the Chicago Medical School. He later graduated from Northwestern University's medical school and remained on its faculty for four years as an anatomy instructor.

PROVIDENT HOSPITAL

In Chicago, as in other parts of the United States, Black doctors and nurses were barred from working in White hospitals and clinics. As a result, many operations performed in the Black community were often done on kitchen tables or worse. Williams founded Provident Hospital in 1891, the nation's first nonracial hospital—a hospital without racial barriers. His hospital created jobs for Black medical professionals. The hospital's focus was on surgery.

Provident Hospital was three stories high and contained only twelve beds when it opened. It had very little money with which to keep its doors open. Volunteers came to the rescue, scrubbing floors, painting walls, and donating money, furniture, sheets, pillows, food, soap, and anything else that was needed.

Williams also founded the first training program for African American nurses. Jessie C. Scales Sleet, a native of Stratford, Ontario, was one of the nurses who trained at Provident Hospital, being graduated in 1895. She followed Williams to Freedmen's Hospital and became the nation's first Black public health nurse in 1900.

THE CORNISH CASE

Williams was not the first person to attempt heart surgery. He was, however, the first to save a patient's life by doing so. Williams's triumph brought nearly instant local fame to him and the hospital. But Williams became ill shortly after the operation and wrote nothing on the procedure. In addition, he was busy taking a post at Freedmen's Hospital at Howard University in Washington, D.C. He didn't write about the operation until 1897. In a weekly journal, *The Medical Record,* his article, "Stab Wound of the Heart and Pericardium—Suture of the Pericardium—Recovery—Patient Alive Three Years Afterward," outlined the case.

By that time the German surgeon Louis Rehn had written of a similar procedure he had successfully completed in 1896. At that time it was Rehn, not Williams, who was credited with the medical breakthrough. Had Williams been White, a controversy would not have existed.

Williams was the first Black on the Illinois Board of Health and a founder and first vice-president of the National Medical Association. In 1913 he was the first Black named a fellow of the American College of Surgeons.

Williams retired from medical practice in 1920 and moved to Idlewild, a summer resort community in Michigan's northern woods. In 1926 the doctor suffered a stroke, from which he never recovered. He died in 1931.

Charles Henry Turner, 1867–1923

Charles Henry Turner was the first person to prove that insects could hear and distinguish pitch and that roaches learn by trial and error. His studies included moths, bees, and other insects, and he was regarded as an authority on the behavior patterns of ants and spiders.

In all, Turner published nearly fifty articles on insect and animal behavior in such journals as the *Zoological Bulletin, Journal of Comparative Neurology, Psychological Bulletin, Journal of Animal Behavior,* and *Biological Bulletin.* He also left behind a partially written book of nature stories for children and a collection of poetry.

Early Innovators

Turner's experimentation on insects at the University of Chicago provided new understanding of how they perceived the world. Through his work on bees, for example, he proved that odor alone did not guide the insects. In a series of experiments he showed that bees were guided by memory as well and that they could distinguish certain colors and patterns. Turner also demonstrated that some insects actually can hear. Working with moths, he found that they respond to sounds within a certain range.

In addition, he showed that cockroaches could find their way through a maze through trial and error. He also was able to break them of their natural behavior of avoiding the light by using electric shocks as a negative reinforcement.

While he spent his time conducting experiments on ants and spiders, he also did research on crayfish and a number of small invertebrates.

Turner's most notable discovery was considered so remarkable within the scientific community that it was named in his honor. The term "Turner's circling" refers to the unique turning movement made by some ants as they try to find the way back to the nest. He also showed how ants depended more on sight to get home than had once been thought.

To demonstrate ant behavior, Turner set up a cardboard platform, attached ramps leading down to an artificial ant nest, and placed columns to deflect light rays. He then put several ants and their eggs, larvae, and pupae on the platform and switched on a light. Through a series of seemingly random wanderings, the ants found their way to the nest.

Turner attached a second ramp, which also led to the nest but from a different direction. The ants ignored it. Testing an accepted theory that ants follow their own scent, he switched the ramps. The ants continued to follow the original path. Once he moved the light, however, the ants resumed their circling behavior.

Turner wrote: "Immediately a remarkable change occurs. The ants act as though they were in a panic. They seemed lost."

After the ants had adjusted to the change in lighting, Turner concluded that light indeed was a significant homing factor.

A FASCINATION WITH INSECTS

Turner was born on February 3, 1867, in Cincinnati, Ohio, where he was reared. His father was a church custodian, and his mother a nurse. Historians say that Turner's father owned an extensive library and that young Charles spent hours poring through the volumes.

As a child he developed an almost fanatical interest in the habits and behavior of insects. He spent many an hour crouched over anthills or perched under a spider's web, carefully watching the movements of insects.

After finishing high school, Turner attended the University of Cincinnati. He earned his bachelor's degree in 1891 and his master's degree the following year. He taught courses at his alma mater for a brief time before leaving the area.

In 1893 he moved to Atlanta, where he taught biology at Clark College for two years. Afterward he held several education-related positions in Georgia, including high school principal and schoolteacher.

After earning his doctorate from the University of Chicago in 1907, Turner never again sought a teaching post at an American university. Turner wanted to teach younger people. He was so committed to this that a year before leaving the University of Chicago, he sent a letter to the principal of a St. Louis high school, which was accompanied by a note from the minister at his church. As a result, Turner became the biology teacher at Sumner High School in St. Louis in 1908 at a starting annual salary of $1,080 and remained there until his death fifteen years later.

Early Innovators

Turner devoted the remainder of his life to teaching, and to conducting his research during his off hours. His class lectures often involved use of a microscope, chalkboard illustrations, and fieldwork. He took his students out on nature hikes, pointing out the varied forms of animal and insect life they encountered.

Observers said that Turner's students had their teacher's undivided attention. When asked once why he had chosen high school over collegiate pursuits at a time when few Blacks of his skill level were even being considered as college instructors, he replied, "I feel that I am needed here and can do much more for my people."

After his death in 1923 the St. Louis Board of Education built a school for physically handicapped Black children and named it in Turner's honor. When the 1954 Supreme Court *Brown* v. *Topeka, Board of Education* decision knocked down the legal segregation of Black and White in schools, the Turner School was converted into a middle school.

Joseph Lee, 1849–1905?

Joseph Lee was a bread specialist, a businessman and a restaurateur in the Boston area. He is credited with the bread-crumbing machine and the bread-making machine.

Born in 1849, Lee held his first job in a bakery when he was just a boy. During the late 1800s Lee owned and managed the Woodland Park Hotel in Newton, Massachusetts, for seventeen years. Prior to that he owned two restaurants.

In 1902 Lee opened the Lee Catering Company, an upscale establishment on Boylston Street on the Back Bay. He also owned and operated the Squantum Inn, located on the South Shore, a classy seafood resort.

Lee, who was regarded as a master cook, was said to have disliked the fact that so much bread was wasted each day because it became stale. His invention of the bread-crumbing machine reduced bread to crumbs by a tearing and grinding process. He used the crumbs to make croquettes, escalloped oysters, cutlets, dressing for poultry, cake batter, fried meats, and puddings. His invention was patented on June 4, 1895.

Lee sold his patent to a New Hampshire manufacturer. The Royal Worcester Bread Crumb Company of Boston made the machine, which became standard equipment in top restaurants around the world.

He later received a second patent for his invention of a machine for making bread. His machine mixed the ingredients and was a more sanitary way to knead dough than by hand. Only one or two people were needed to operate the machine, which could turn out hundreds of loaves a day, as opposed to more than two dozen people performing the task by hand. Variations on his original design are still in use.

It is believed that Lee died in 1905.

J. W. Benton, 1800s

Benton received a patent on October 2, 1890, for his creation of a derrick for hoisting heavy weights. The Kentucky-born inventor was said to have walked the entire distance to Washington, D.C., to see about his patent.

Sarah Boone, 1800s

Boone came up with an idea for a narrow wooden board, with collapsible leg supports and covered with padding, in 1892. Prior to her ironing board, this task normally required taking a plank and placing it between two chairs or simply using the dining table.

Henry A. Bowman, 1800s

Henry Bowman, a Worcester, Massachusetts, native, patented his flag-making process in February 1892. However, he was unable to hire an attorney to help him protect it when a New York company stole the idea. Bowman left the flag-making business, and nothing further is known about him.

Shearman Butteese, 1870–?

Born on May 15, 1870, in Richmond, Texas, Butteese is said to have invented the E.Z. Adjustable Sides, movable sidewalls used on wheelbarrows and trucks.

Butteese's schooling included public schools in Richmond and Harrisburg, Texas, and the Houston Methodist Seminary.

Robert Lee Campbell, 1875–?

Credited with developing a steam engine valve gear, Campbell was both a teacher and a soldier.

Campbell was born on March 3, 1875, in Athens, Georgia. He was graduated in engineering from the Tuskegee Institute in 1895 and studied mathematics and science through the American School of Correspondence.

His teaching credentials include stints at Alabama A&M University in Huntsville (1902 to 1912); Western University in Kansas City, Kansas (1911); and North Carolina A&T University (1913 to 1917 and 1919 to 1930).

Between 1899 and 1901, during the Spanish-American War, Campbell served in the Forty-ninth Volunteer Infantry, achieving the rank of sergeant. He began the First World War as a first lieutenant in 1917 and was recommended for promotion to captain following the Battle of Argonne.

Shelby J. Davidson, 1868–?

Born on May 10, 1868, in Lexington, Kentucky, Davidson is credited with inventing a mechanical tabulator that may have been a forerunner to the modern adding machine. Davidson was graduated from Howard University in 1893.

William Augustus Hinton, 1883–1959

Hinton was the co-creator of the Davies-Hinton blood and spinal fluid test in collaboration with Dr. J.A.V. Davies, as well as the originator of the Hinton test for syphilis, still in use in some parts of the world.

Born in Chicago on December 15, 1883, Hinton earned both his bachelor's degree (1905) and his M.D. (1912) from Harvard University. After graduation, Hinton spent three years as a volunteer assistant at Boston's Massachusetts General Hospital. From 1916 to 1924 he held research posts with the Boston Dispensary and at the Massachusetts Department of Public Health. Hinton received a lecturer's position at Harvard Medical School in 1925. He remained there, teaching preventative medicine and hygiene, until 1952. He was the first non-White named to a full professorship at Harvard Medical in 1949.

In 1931 Hinton created a medical technician school for poor girls. The school eventually grew into one of the largest in the nation for training technicians.

So afraid was Hinton of having his work rejected if his race was widely known that he refused the 1938 Spingarn Award given by Howard University for Black excellence. He died in Canton, Massachusetts, in 1959.

Robert A. Pelham, Jr., 1859–1943

Pelham's inventions included a pasting machine, a tabulator that was used in the census count of manufacturers, and a tallying machine that was used to count populations.

Early Innovators

Born on January 4, 1859, near Petersburg, Virginia, Pelham wrote for the Detroit *Free Press* from 1884 to 1891.

Alabama Vest, 1800s

According to historians, Vest is the originator of the kazoo, based on the mirliton, a pipelike instrument brought to America by Africans. Sometime during the 1840s, Vest had kazoos made to his specifications by Thaddeus Von Clegg and exhibited them in a fair in Atlanta. The instrument was known in those days as the Down South Submarine.

THE TWENTIETH CENTURY

George Washington Carver, 1860–1943

George Washington Carver's accomplishments with the sweet potato and other southern plants lifted a nation desperate to prove that the Horatio Alger success story applied to anyone—even Blacks. During his lifetime the botanist and former slave was lavished with honors from such notables as automaker Henry Ford, inventor Thomas A. Edison, and President Franklin D. Roosevelt. He was the subject of Hollywood film lore—the stuff of which legends were made.

Carver's scientific discoveries include more than three hundred different products derived from the peanut, some one hundred from sweet potatoes, about seventy-five from the pecan, and many more from Georgia clay. He became an authority on plant diseases throughout the South and worldwide.

His boyhood farm home in Missouri is now a national monument.

CARVER'S LEGEND

In many ways Carver's work with the sweet potato lives on. Today, responding to the world hunger crisis and the demands of health-conscious consumers, agriculturalists and nutritionists are finding new uses for the versatile vegetable.

In the same brick building where Carver conducted his research, today's Tuskegee researchers use gene guns to alter the DNA of sweet potatoes. They hope to field-test sweet potatoes containing a synthetic gene that can boost the vegetable's protein content. Under a NASA contract, Tuskegee scientists have developed a way of growing sweet potatoes without soil, using a nutrient-laden plastic membrane to nourish sweet potato vines for months at a time. Other laboratories are designing sweet potatoes that can resist the crop-destroying sweet potato weevil.

Recently, researchers from twenty countries who came to Tuskegee to discuss the future of the sweet potato said the roots are rich in vitamin A and packed with vitamin C, vitamin E, riboflavin, thiamin, niacin, iron, and calcium. A half-cup of sweet potatoes even has as much fiber as a bran muffin.

In Japan, sweet potato roots are used to brew shochu, an alcoholic beverage. In China, sweet potatoes are the source of starch for cooking noodles. And in Africa, the carotene-rich roots and leaves provide much-needed vitamin A, the lack of which has led to blindness in children in a number of underdeveloped countries.

To honor Carver's one-hundred twenty-fifth birthday, Tuskegee even made a deal to market "Tuskegee Chunk"— peanut butter and chocolate ice cream.

HERO OR VILLAIN?

Some of his contemporaries saw Carver not as hero but as an embarrassment. They thought he was a symbol of Black excellence propped up by someone else as a role model for the Black community.

Carver once said that he saw himself as something of a savior of the Black race when he arrived at Alabama's Tuskegee Institute and that he could not understand what he called the jealousy of his fellow professors. Some have said that Carver and Tuskegee founder Booker T. Washington also clashed on several occasions, with Washington being the more practical of the two, while Carver was more concerned with being left alone to conduct his experiments.

Many Black colleagues criticized what they called Carver's willingness to pander to whites to the detriment of his Black students. One Tuskegee Institute professor once commented that Carver "never taught a Black person anything" and accused the scientist of lording his fame in the White community over his peers.

Other Black scholars came to Carver's defense, however, saying that the scientist possessed a genius by scholars of any race. Throughout his life, and well after his death, debate raged over the quality of his accomplishments and his place in African American history.

A work by artist Robert Colescott only added to the controversy over the scientist's place in history. The portrait depicts Carver, standing in for George Washington, crossing the Delaware River in a rowboat along with a banjo-pickin' minstrel, a plump Aunt Jemima, and other Black images fostered and revered by White society. "The painting is about tokenism," said Colescott, adding that Carver had been one of the few Blacks mentioned in the history textbooks of his childhood. "Carver was allowed to be noble, but it was a crumb in terms of what was available."

REMEMBRANCES

In February 1991, Iowa State University honored the Carver legacy one hundred years after he first set foot on the

Ames campus. Several Iowa State alums, who had seen Carver while they were students at Tuskegee University, recalled their encounters with the scientist during his final days at the Alabama school.

Helen Wilson Bratcher was one of a number of Black Tuskegee students who flocked around Carver as he made his way across campus. She spoke of him as a man who constantly encouraged students, telling them they could be whatever they wanted. "For a bunch of young Black students in the 1940s, we needed that encouragement," said Bratcher. Bratcher was so impressed by Carver that she also enrolled at Iowa State University. "When I was ready to leave Tuskegee, I said, 'Carver went to Iowa State? OK, then I'll go to Iowa State. If he did it, it's good enough for me,' " she said.

Cecile Hoover Edwards never met Carver during her days as a Tuskegee student. She was a fifteen-year-old freshman in economics when she approached the doors of the Carver museum in the early 1940s. Too shy to knock, she instead went around to a window and peered in, hoping to gain a glance at him. She remembered seeing only his hands, hard at work in the lab. It was enough for her.

"The impact of seeing those hands is something I have never forgotten," said Edwards.

RAGS TO RICHES

Carver was born into bondage in 1860 on German immigrant Moses Carver's thirty-two-acre plantation near Diamond Grove, Missouri. Little is known of Carver's father except that he had been kept on a nearby farm and died in an accident before young Carver's birth.

According to legend, almost immediately after Carver's birth, he and his mother were kidnapped by slave raiders, who had infested much of the Midwest. The deathly ill Carver was ransomed back to slaveowner Moses Carver in exchange for a racehorse, valued at three hundred dollars. Though some scholars believe she continued to live somewhere in or near Kansas, Carver never saw his mother again.

Carver was a frail child and unable to handle hard physical work. Many believe his childhood illnesses damaged the scientist's vocal cords, leaving him with an extremely high-pitched voice. Instead of doing the type of work reserved for slaves, Carver was assigned less physically taxing chores, which included caring for the plants around the plantation.

"My education was picked up here and there," Carver later said. "Mr. and Mrs. Carver taught me to read, spell and write just a little."

His earliest formal education came in a one-room schoolhouse located a few miles from the plantation. A Black couple named Andrew and Mariah Watkins lived near the school and became a second family to the eleven-year-old, encouraging his study of plants. He later spoke well of the Watkinses in letters and essays.

Despite his intelligence, he was refused admission to a White high school in Kansas that previously had accepted him sight unseen. "No Blacks allowed," he was told. He eventually enrolled at a high school in Minneapolis, Kansas, where he earned a diploma.

Carver drifted for a time through Kansas and Missouri, filling such odd jobs as cook, laundry worker, and farmhand. For a time he stopped in Olathe and Ness County, Kansas. All the while he sought to know more. Of his travels, he later wrote: "From a child, I had an inordinate desire for knowledge, especially music and painting, flowers and the sciences, algebra being one of my favorite studies."

BOTANY

Carver was thirty years old in 1890 when he enrolled as a freshman—and the first Black student—at Simpson College in

Indianola, Iowa. Carver recalled being reluctant to apply to another college after he had been rejected by Highland College in Kansas. No Blacks allowed. At Simpson, Carver devoted himself to the study of a wide range of subjects, from botany to music to art, which became a lifelong personal passion. He had developed a level excellence with his drawings and managed to exhibit some of his works at the 1893 world's fair in Chicago, where they earned honorable mention. Still, his art teacher at Simpson, Etta Budd, encouraged him to choose science over art.

Botany consumed the life of the man who came to be known as the plant doctor. In 1891, with Budd's help, he transferred to the Iowa State College of Agriculture and Mechanical Arts in Ames (which became Iowa State University), becoming the first African to attend. Budd's father was head of the horticulture department. Carver studied botany, agricultural chemistry, geometry, bacteriology, zoology, and entomology.

As an assistant botanist at a college experiment station he was the university's first Black teacher. He developed his skills in plant pathology and mycology, the branch of botany concerned with fungi.

While he described his experiences at Iowa State as positive, Carver admitted to having experienced the sting of racism. His tone, however, seemed more like an apology for his own ethnicity than an indictment of those who disliked him. When he first arrived at the school, for example, Carver found that none of the White students would share a room with him. "Being a colored boy, and the crowded condition of the school, made it rather embarrassing for some, and made the question of a room rather puzzling," he wrote.

To earn money, Carver waited tables in the school's dining room, did janitorial work, and worked as a masseur for the sports teams. But he was refused service at the dining room and had to eat his meals with the Black field hands in the basement. One woman walked out of the dining room rather than be served by him. Another time he was assigned to escort the governor to a school banquet to avoid his having to escort a White woman.

Carver earned his bachelor's degree in 1894 and his master's degree in 1896. The latter year he was awarded an honorary doctorate from the University of Rochester.

TUSKEGEE AND BOOKER T. WASHINGTON

Also in 1896 Carver accepted the famed Washington's invitation to teach at the Tuskegee Normal and Industrial Institute in Alabama. He was named director of the agriculture department. He also was to serve as director of the agricultural experiment station, which had been authorized by the Alabama legislature. Carver spent the remainder of his life there.

Carver's fascination with crops went well beyond just a love of plants. It developed from a desire to help others use to the utmost whatever resources they had. Carver eventually won the confidence of the farmers by showing them how to rotate their crops to save the soil. Cotton, the dominant cash crop in the South for two hundred years, had badly damaged the soil, rendering it nearly useless. Carver told farmers that by planting peas, peanuts, sweet potatoes, soybeans, pecans, and clover they could replenish the earth because these crops put needed nutrients back into the soil.

Among Carver's synthetic creations from plants were adhesives, axle grease, bleach, buttermilk, cheese, chili sauce, cream, dyes, flour, fuel briquettes, ink, instant coffee, insulating board, linoleum, mayonnaise, meat tenderizer, metal polish, milk flakes, mucilage, paper, salve, shampoo, shoe polish, shaving cream, steak sauce, sugar, marble, rubber, talcum powder, vanishing cream, wood stain, and wood filler.

While Carver did discover many uses for peanuts, peanut butter was not one of them. Peanut butter was first made by an unnamed St. Louis physician, who in 1890 put peanuts through

81

a meat grinder. The doctor gave the paste to his patients as a high-protein, easily digestible food.

During the late 1920s and early 1930s Carver's reputation as a Horatio Alger in Blackface began to grow worldwide. His timing could not have been much better. It was the era of heroes such as baseball slugger Babe Ruth and the '27 Yankees. It was flappers, the end of Prohibition, and Charles Lindbergh crossing the Atlantic Ocean by plane.

It was the era of the segregated Negro Baseball League and the Homestead Grays. It was the Harlem Renaissance, jazz, and Langston Hughes; Black scholars Washington and W.E.B. Du Bois squaring off over strategies for African liberation.

Then came the Depression. Carver's peanut creations were the perfect answer for a country needing to stretch its limited resources.

By 1938 peanuts had become a two-hundred-million-dollar industry and the number one product in Alabama.

HONORS AND AWARDS

That same year Simpson College honored Carver with one of many honorary doctorates he was to receive. As his reputation grew, he seemed to live somewhere between two separate worlds. He was at once the stuff of legends for those who wanted to believe in an American dream and the object of scorn for those who saw him as selling out his people in the name of personal glory. Yet the honors kept coming. Tuskegee unveiled a bust of Carver in 1937, and a year later a feature film, *The Life of George Washington Carver*, opened in Hollywood. In 1941 longtime friend Henry Ford dedicated the Carver Museum at Tuskegee. The following year Selma University awarded Carver a Ph.D., and he received the Roosevelt Medal for Outstanding Contribution to Southern Agriculture.

During his forty-six years at Tuskegee, Carver worked virtually alone. He died on January 5, 1943, and was buried on

Tuskegee's campus near the grave of Booker T. Washington. Prior to his death, the botanist directed that thirty-three thousand dollars he had saved be used to establish the George Washington Carver Foundation. The research organization exists today.

In 1955 a monument was dedicated to Carver's memory near Diamond Grove, Missouri. He was the first Black American scientist so honored. The following year Simpson College dedicated a science building in his honor. In 1957 a Polaris submarine bearing his name was christened in Newport News, Virginia.

Other honors include his being named a fellow of the Royal Society of Arts in 1917; his having his likeness on a postage stamp in 1947 and on a fifty-cent piece in 1951; the dedication of Carver Hall, complete with a statue, in 1968; election to the Kansas City, Kansas, Agricultural Hall of Fame of Great Americans in 1977; and induction into the National Inventors Hall of Fame in 1990.

Though it was reported that Carver never patented his discoveries, he actually held three patents for two products produced in his lab: for cosmetics in 1925, for a paint and stain process in 1925, and for paint process and production in 1927.

Matthew A. Henson, 1866–1955

Olive Henson, in her sixties, recalled her childhood with great fondness, particularly the family trips to New York to visit her great-uncle Matthew A. Henson. Pictures of Henson's Arctic trips covered the walls of his home, Olive recalled. Often he took out the maps to show her where he and Rear Admiral Robert E. Peary had been.

But when Olive returned to her home in Boston and told her teachers about the family hero, she was met by disbelief.

"They'd say it wasn't so because it wasn't written in the history books. But my father said, 'It's OK—we know the truth,' " she said.

THE EXPLORER

Matthew Alexander Henson, an explorer, was the first known human to reach the North Pole. Together with Admiral Peary, he is regarded as the preeminent explorer of the Arctic.

Peary, tired and hurting from the loss of most of his toes to frostbite, chose Henson to go ahead to make the final leg of the expedition. Henson went ahead to make final calculations and await Peary's arrival. Henson arrived at the Pole via sled on April 6, 1909, forty-five minutes ahead of his fellow explorer. When the rest of the expedition arrived, Henson was given the honor of planting the U.S. flag on the site.

Henson was born on August 6, 1866, one year after the end of the Civil War, on a farm in Nanjemay, Charles County, Maryland, once used as a slave market. His parents, Lemuel and Caroline, died when he was eight years old. At age eleven, young Matthew ran away from a foster mother he later said had been cruel to him and set out on his own to find an uncle who lived in nearby Washington, D.C.

For a time Henson's uncle sent him to school, but that soon ended because the uncle could no longer care for his nephew. Young Henson took a job washing dishes in a Washington restaurant. There he eavesdropped as guests spoke of the sea, the docks in Baltimore, and of adventure.

YOUTHFUL WORLD TRAVELER

At thirteen Henson signed on in Baltimore as a cabin boy on a ship bound for Hong Kong. Captain Childs's chambers became his classroom, as the captain taught him reading, writing, mathematics, seamanship, navigation, geography, and first aid. Childs was a father figure for Henson and his only real teacher.

Henson, who eventually became a full-fledged seaman, loved the sea and spent five years sailing to North Africa, Japan, China, the Philippines, Spain, France, and over the Black Sea to Russia. Henson later said that his world travels introduced him to different languages and peoples. During a winter trip to Russia, for example, he learned how to speak Russian, hunt wolves, and drive sleighs.

When Childs died at sea, Henson left the ship and went to Newfoundland. He then caught a fishing boat to Boston, Providence, and New York City, working odd jobs along the way. He was seventeen.

HENSON AND PEARY

At nineteen he returned to Washington, where he got a job as a stock clerk for Steinmetz and Sons, Hatters and Furriers, a men's clothing store. He was in the back room of the store in 1887 taking inventory when Peary entered the store in search of a sun helmet. The store owner introduced the two, and Peary soon offered Henson a servant's job on an expedition to Nicaragua, which Henson accepted.

Peary had recently returned from Central America, where he had served as a civil engineer for the U.S. Navy. He had gone to Nicaragua to map out a route for a canal to connect the Atlantic and Pacific oceans. In 1886, one year earlier, Peary had begun to explore the Arctic by way of Greenland, where he spent months studying the coast.

Anxious to finance a second trip to Greenland, Peary arrived in Washington. There were no takers for his Arctic plan, and he focused himself on his assignment to the south. Surveying the location for a canal took several months. During that time Henson rose in the ranks to field assistant, thus beginning a twenty-three-year association between the two men. Peary told Henson of his wish to explore Greenland further and reach the North Pole.

On their return to Washington, Peary asked Henson to join him on a trip to Greenland, despite his not having the funds to support their expedition. Henson agreed. Henson later said that the opportunity to travel the globe meant more than a desire for adventure. He also wanted to prove that his courage, intelligence, and will were the equal of anyone else's.

ARCTIC ADVENTURE

In June 1891 Henson and Peary started out on the first of what were six trips to the Arctic between 1891 and 1908. A crew of seven left New York: Peary, his wife, Henson, a doctor, a geologist, a bird watcher, and a skier. Their provisions and equipment included pea soup, biscuits, fruit and dried beef; cooking apparatus; sleeping bags and tents; scientific instruments, thermometers, compasses, a sextant, a barometer, and camera equipment.

By late July the party had reached Greenland's McCormick Bay, where they were to return in a year to meet up with the ship. Henson turned his attention to building a wooden house for the party to live in and dogsleds to traverse the snow. By trading guns and bullets to the locals, they were able to purchase the dogs.

Only Peary and the skier went on the first trip once the winter snows had passed. Henson spent his time among the Eskimos, learning their language and customs. The skills he had acquired in Russia served him well in the ice and snow.

By the middle of August 1892, when the ship arrived to get the party, Peary and the skier had not yet returned. Finally, the two did come back, exhausted, frozen, and near starvation, from their twelve-hundred-mile journey across Greenland.

Back in the United States, Peary and Henson were sought after for a national lecture tour. They were instant celebrities.

Yet they had not accomplished the one goal they both now shared: reaching the North Pole.

THE SECOND TRIP

In June 1893 Peary, his wife, Henson, and a crew of eight left New York, again amid media hoopla and high expectations. They reached Greenland the following month and built a house near Bowdoin Bay in preparation for winter. Small parties went ahead during the fall, burying supplies in the snow that would be picked up by the full expedition as it passed in the spring. The locations were marked by long poles, driven into the ice and snow.

The winter at Bowdoin Bay was harsh, wiping out many needed supplies. But in March 1894 Peary's party set off for the north. The temperature reached forty degrees below zero at one point. That and howling winds caused the deaths of some of the crew. Others were badly injured by frostbite. The party returned to base. This time it was not meant to be.

Only Peary, Henson, and a journalist decided to remain another winter when the ship for America returned. The three men traveled more than 450 miles into Greenland the next April with three sleds and thirty-seven dogs. They got no farther as the rugged countryside made travel more dangerous. Thirty-six dogs were lost, some used for food when supplies ran out.

When Henson and Peary returned to New York, however, they were not empty-handed. Two of three meteorites that had fallen on Greenland years before were loaded onto the ship. The third meteor, weighing more than seventy tons, was too large to carry. The meteors were put on display at New York's American Museum of Natural History.

The explorers also loaded animal hides and animal specimens captured by Henson. The New York museum hired Henson to work in its taxidermy department, where he spent the next two years. He was responsible for mounting the walrus skins he had collected and arranging lifelike nature exhibits. He also designed Eskimo village replicas.

In 1897 Henson and Peary returned to Greenland to retrieve the third meteor, said at that time to be the largest known meteor in the world. It, too, now resides in the New York museum.

Henson was still at the museum in 1898, when Peary returned from receiving both a medal from the Royal Geographical Society and a ship in which to sail north yet again.

Peary had come under criticism from some Whites for wanting Henson to join him on his next expedition and was under pressure to choose a White man. Such was the thinking during this era, a Plessy vs. Ferguson "separate but equal" world, where Whites built legal and social walls to exclude Blacks. It was a cruel reality in this country.

In those days civil rights organizations sought to draw attention to the lynching of Blacks by White mobs, which had reached epidemic proportions nationally as the result of governmental indifference. (The National Association for the Advancement of Colored People did not even exist; it was founded in Buffalo, New York, one year after Henson and Peary finally reached the North Pole.)

For his part, Henson had begun to enjoy New York life and was even considering marriage. But by the end of the year the two men, accompanied only by a doctor, set off on yet another voyage.

SEARCHING FOR THE WAY NORTH

The trio spent the next four years searching for a passage to the North Pole. Earlier they had discovered that Greenland was indeed an island connected to the north by sheets of ice, not the solid landmass for which they had hoped.

In 1899 they traveled on foot to deserted Fort Conger,

located about four hundred miles from the Pole. Peary's toes became frostbitten during the journey. Seven were removed by the doctor, causing them to abandon plans to head northward until he healed.

Peary had recovered by the spring, and he, Henson, and one Eskimo set out again. Peary's feet made travel slow, and they turned back. It was two years before they tried again.

With a crew of seven Eskimos, they made only sixty miles before again being forced back. They returned to New York in August 1902, exhausted and defeated.

Peary spent the next three years designing a ship powerful enough to cut through the ice of the Arctic Ocean, while Henson worked as a porter for the Pennsylvania Railroad.

With the new ship ready to go, Peary, Henson, and a small crew tried one more time in July 1905. By September the new ship had taken them farther north than anyone had ever gone. They stopped at a spot five hundred miles from their goal and settled in for the winter. In the spring they left with a crew of 22 Eskimo men, 20 sleds, and more than 130 dogs.

Henson was the lead person, charting a path and leaving supplies along the way. Despite melting ice, open water, and severe storms, they got to within 125 miles of the Pole. No one had ever gone farther.

They returned to New York on Christmas Eve 1906 in a ship that had been battered and broken by the icy Arctic elements. Peary considered making this his last voyage, but in 1907 the Peary Arctic Club offered to support him one last time.

During the lull in waiting for the ship to be repaired, Henson was invited by a Mrs. Gardner of Harlem to a dinner party in his honor. There he met and fell immediately in love with Lucy Ross. They were married in 1907, a year later. After the honeymoon Henson turned his attention to supervising the ship's repairs.

89

SAILING INTO HISTORY

Peary, Henson, and five others left New York for the 1908 expedition. The ship had been renamed in honor of then President Theodore Roosevelt. The party made a brief stop at Oyster Bay, Long Island, to meet the President, then again set sail for Greenland.

The party reached Etah Harbor on August 12. Forty-nine Eskimo men, women, and children accompanied them northward. They reached Cape Sheridan and began sending supplies ahead to Cape Columbia, some ninety miles to the north. In his journal Henson later commented that the winter winds reached such strength that they picked up boulders weighing up to one hundred pounds and hurled them as far as one hundred feet.

On February 18, 1909, Henson and his crew left Cape Sheridan and headed north. Through cold, through wind, over rough terrain, Henson's crew arrived at Cape Columbia and teamed up with another crew that had arrived much earlier. Peary arrived later. Henson and four Eskimos—Ootah, Eqinqwah, Seegloo, and Ooqueah—set out for the Pole on March 1. Four other groups also set out. Each was to take turns, systematically passing the others while they slept and forging a trail ahead, according to Peary's plan.

On March 14 one party was sent back to Cape Columbia. Temperatures had reached sixty degrees below zero. Others were sent back. Soon they were within 133 miles of the North Pole. On April 4 they were within 60 miles; the next day, 35. Since no sextant was accurate enough to gauge the exact location of the pole, experts agreed that getting within 10 to 20 miles of the general area would be close enough to claim success in reaching it.

On April 6 Henson reached a point that he believed was close to the North Pole. About forty-five minutes later Peary arrived. Their instruments told them that they were within ninety degrees of their goal. They had done it. They had discovered what for them was earth's last great frontier. Henson triumphantly planted the American flag on top of the world.

In 1912 another group of explorers, inspired by Peary and Henson, set foot on the South Pole.

SUCCESS AND ANONYMITY

This time the return to New York was sweet. Henson toured the country, lecturing on his exploits, while Peary prepared a paper to present to the National Geographic Survey. At the end of his tour Henson wrote *A Negro at the North Pole*, detailing his adventure.

At first Dr. Frederick Cook, a rival of Peary's, falsely claimed that he had arrived at the pole before Henson and Peary. The claim was discredited, but Peary died a short time later, and Henson was ignored.

Six years after his famous trip to the pole, Henson was working in a parking garage. President William H. Taft had made Peary an admiral, but Henson was not recognized until 1913, following an appeal by Black leaders in New York. A Black politician helped him secure a job as messenger boy in the U.S. Customs House at a salary of two thousand dollars a year. Henson stayed there until he retired at seventy.

Four separate bills in 1926, 1936, 1938, and 1949 in the U.S. Congress that would have granted a pension to Henson were defeated. Even the cook on Admiral Byrd's mission to the South Pole had been awarded pension money, and each expedition member had received a gold medal from Congress. The federal legislature finally bowed somewhat to outside pressure, awarding gold medals to the entire Peary party. A year later they all received the Navy Medal.

In 1950 President Harry S Truman was among those gathered to honor Henson in a Pentagon ceremony. Four years later

President Dwight D. Eisenhower received Henson at the White House, then accompanied him to Arlington Cemetery to lay a wreath on Peary's grave.

Henson died on March 9, 1955, and was buried in New York City.

THE SONS OF THE EXPLORERS

Peary and Henson shared more than skills as explorers of the Arctic. They also shared a secret that strengthened their bond. In 1906 each fathered a child by an Eskimo woman.

In May 1987 Ahnahkaq Henson and Karree Peary, the half Eskimo sons of the two explorers, traveled to the United States for a first-ever meeting with their American relatives. The explorers' sons visited the Peary grave at Arlington National Cemetery and met Henson and Peary relatives in Maine, Massachusetts, New York, and Maryland.

For the two men, both in their eighties, the trip was their first away from the cold of northwestern Greenland. America was a far cry from Qaanaaq, the northernmost continuously inhabited area on earth, located a mere 850 miles from the North Pole.

The parentage of the two men was always known to the Eskimos. French ethnologist Jean Malaurie first reported of their existence after a visit to Greenland in the 1950s, and Harvard University scholar S. Allen Counter later wrote of them in a magazine article. But in the America of that day such a disclosure would have ruined the memory of Peary, who died in 1920. During his lifetime, Peary had been criticized for his association with Henson.

Counter, an associate professor of neurophysiology at Harvard University, has studied Henson's life as part of a project, begun in 1970, tracing the influence of Blacks in world history. He first heard of dark-skinned Eskimos, known as Kulnocktoko, from Scandinavian colleagues in 1977. Since the only

Black man Counter knew to have interacted with the Eskimos was Henson, he decided to check it out.

MAI PALUK

In August 1986 Counter flew by helicopter to Siropolu, Greenland, then traveled by boat to Inglefield Bay with two Eskimos. He asked people he met about the Kulnocktoko and was directed to a modest house. Counter walked up to the house and through an interpreter told the elderly man he met at the door that he was looking for the son of "Mai Paluk." The old man laughed and told the professor that his search was over. In an even more remote village Counter later found Karree.

Henson's nickname among the Eskimos was Mai Paluk, or "dark-faced one." Some Eskimos had assumed that Henson was himself Eskimo because he was so dark.

On June 29, 1987, shortly after returning from America, Ahnahkaq died of cancer, in Moriusaq, Greenland. Ahnahkaq had five children and twenty-two grandchildren. Karree had five children and eighteen grandchildren.

On April 6, 1988, Counter, the Henson family, and others succeeded in getting the bodies of Henson and his wife moved from New York and reinterred at Arlington National Cemetery, next to Peary's grave. Guion Bluford, the first American Black to venture into outer space, gave the ceremonial eulogy.

Among the honors Henson received were master of science degrees from Morgan State and Howard universities and recognition from the U.S. Congress, the Explorers Club, and the Department of Defense. A building at New Orleans's Dillard University and a Chicago public school are named for him.

A plaque honoring his codiscovery of the North Pole was unveiled at the Maryland statehouse in Annapolis in 1961. The inscription on a gold medal from the Chicago Geographical Society reads: " 'I can't get along without him'—Peary."

Created Equal

Garrett Augustus Morgan, 1877–1963

Garrett Augustus Morgan is best known for his invention of the automatic traffic signal. He also is the inventor of the gas mask, used by firemen in the early 1900s and by soldiers in World War I.

Morgan was born on March 4, 1877, in Paris, Kentucky, the seventh of eleven children. Elizabeth Reed Morgan, his mother, was a former slave of mixed African and Native tribal blood, who gained her freedom in 1863. Sydney Morgan, his father, was a mulatto.

Morgan's formal education ended nearly as quickly as it began. He left school after the fifth grade, when he was fourteen. He then left home and went to Cincinnati, landing a job in a sewing machine shop and working as a general handyman for a white landowner.

CLEVELAND, OHIO

Morgan moved on again, this time to Cleveland, where he spent the rest of his life. It was 1895. He was broke but knew enough about sewing machines to secure a machine adjuster's job first with the Roots and McBride Company and later with several other firms. His first invention was a sewing machine belt fastener, which he sold for fifty dollars in 1901.

In 1907 Morgan opened his own sewing machine sales and repair shop. He earned enough to buy a home and send for his mother after his father died in 1908. That same year he married Mary Ann Hassek, with whom he shared his life for fifty-five years until his death. Their union was happy and produced three sons.

In 1909 Morgan opened a tailoring shop, which made suits, coats, and dresses. He had about thirty employees in the plant. A practical need brought about the creation of an inven-

94

tion that turned out to have uses not related to sewing. In his shop the needles sewing fabric together moved so quickly that their friction scorched the woolen thread. While Morgan experimented at home on a lubricant to reduce the friction, he inadvertently wiped the substance onto a loose piece of coarse pony-fur cloth. When he returned to his workshop, he noticed that the hairs where he had rubbed his hands were straight.

Out of curiosity, Morgan applied the solution to the hair of his neighbor's pet Airedale, then to his own hair. The cream he created and patented became the G. A. Morgan hair refining cream and was the first human hair straightener. The G. A. Morgan Refining Company, formed in 1913 to sell the cream, did a brisk business and still is located in Cleveland.

THE GAS MASK

Financially secure, Morgan focused his attention on other ideas. Noting the danger faced by firemen overcome by fumes, dust, and smoke, Morgan developed an apparatus in 1912 that he called a safety hood or breathing device. Perhaps his invention was inspired by New York's deadly Triangle Waist Company fire. The 1911 blaze claimed the lives of 146 workers who were trapped inside the factory.

Morgan's crude contraption consisted of a hood, to be placed over a person's head, and a long tube running from the hood to the floor, below the level of smoke in a room. The lower end of the tube was lined with absorbent material, which was moistened before each use to cool the air and prevent dust and smoke from being sucked up into the mask. The device had a second tube to handle exhaled air.

"The object of the invention is to provide a portable attachment which will enable a fireman to enter a house filled with thick suffocating gases and smoke," Morgan said. The device would allow a fire fighter to "perform his duties of saving life and valuables without danger to himself from suffocation."

95

Later known as a gas mask, it was more efficient and reliable than respiratory devices available at the time. The invention was patented in 1914. Once Morgan had modified the device to carry its own air supply, it became useful to soldiers.

The invention spawned the foundation of the National Safety Device Company, of which Morgan was general manager, the only non-White officer in the company. Though Morgan pleaded with Blacks to buy shares in the company, which sold for $10 each, there were no takers. Within a month the value of each share had risen to $100; two years later it was worth more than $250 and was no longer available.

Morgan's mask began to make the rounds nationally as exhibitions and publicity stunts were staged to demonstrate its effectiveness. In 1914 a man walked through a tent filled with the fumes of tar, sulfur, formaldehyde, and manure, which had been set ablaze. After twenty minutes the man walked out of the foul-smelling tent unharmed.

Later the same stunt was attempted at an artificial ice-producing plant, which commonly makes use of the highly toxic gas ammonia. Dry ammonia was pumped into a sealed small room. The demonstrator remained in the room fifteen minutes without a problem.

Morgan received the first grand prize solid gold medal for his invention at the Second International Exposition of Safety and Sanitation in New York. Again, successful demonstrations were given, including one unplanned demonstration, as New York firemen enlisted the devices to rescue victims of a subway disaster.

CRIB NUMBER FIVE

On July 25, 1916, crib number five, a tunnel under construction on Cleveland's Lake Erie exploded, leaving Cleveland Water Works crew members trapped 250 feet below the lake. Many suffocated as the tunnel quickly filled with gas and

Lewis Howard Latimer was a pioneer in the development of the electric light bulb and was the only Black member of Thomas A. Edison's research team of noted scientists.

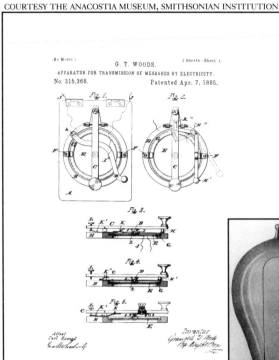

Granville T. Woods was known as the "Black Edison." This signaling device was one of his more than one hundred fifty patents.

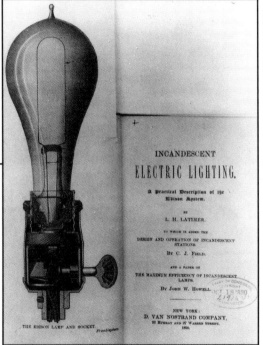

Lewis Latimer and fellow inventor Joseph V. Nichols created the first incandescent light bulb with a carbon filament. Prior to this breakthrough, filament was made from paper, which was more fragile.

Garrett A. Morgan's traffic light

Ralph Gardner was one of more than a dozen Black scientists who were involved in research on the Manhattan Project, which resulted in the creation of the atomic bomb.

Granville T. Woods won two electrical patent battles against Thomas A. Edison. The losses prompted Edison to offer Woods a job, which he refused.

Explorer Matthew Alexander Henson was the first known human to set foot on the North Pole as a member of Admiral Robert E. Peary's expedition.

Elijah McCoy's automatic oiling devices became so universal that no heavy-duty machinery was considered adequate without "the real McCoy," an expression that has become part of the American idiom.

Madame C. J. Walker built a Black cosmetics empire with such products as Wonderful Hair Grower, Superfine face powder, and Glossine pressing oil.

Sarah Breedlove McWilliams
Madame "C. J." Walker

SAMUEL LUMSDEN,

Manufacturer of

GENTLEMEN'S BOOTS AND SHOES,

No. 239 MAIN STREET, BETWEEN FIFTH AND SIXTH,

CINCINNATI.

First Premium Boots.

MECHANICS' INSTITUTE, June 27th, 1840.

The first Premium for Boots was awarded to Samuel Lumsden by Samuel Martin, John Hudson, Jesse O'Niell, Henry Sanders, Henry M'Grew, Matthew Redman, Charles Thomas, Judges.

HENRY BOYD,

MANUFACTURER OF

PATENTED RIGHT & LEFT

Wood Screw and Swelled Rail

BEDSTEADS,

NORTH WEST CORNER OF BROADWAY & EIGHTH STREETS,

CINCINNATI,

Would respectfully inform all those who wish to purchase a superior article of furniture in BEDSTEADS, to call at the wareroom of the subscriber, corner of Broadway and Eighth Streets, and examine for themselves. This newly invented Bedstead is warranted to be superior to any other ever offered in the West :—possessing the following decided advantages over all others heretofore in use :—they can be put up or taken apart in one fourth the time that is required to do the same with others, without the possibility of a mistake ;—are more firm and less apt to become loose and worthless, and without a single harbor for vermin. As soon as their superiority over the common kind becomes known and duly appreciated, they must of necessity take the place of those now in use.

Henry Boyd and other Black carpenters used their skills as a way out of slavery. Boyd's bedstead shop in Cincinnati was among that city's more successful furniture manufacturers.

Sailmaker James Forten lived in an era in which Africans were an integral part of the American adventure on the high seas. In 1776, about one fifth of the merchant seamen in Philadelphia were free Africans. By 1846, there were roughly six thousand Black seamen.

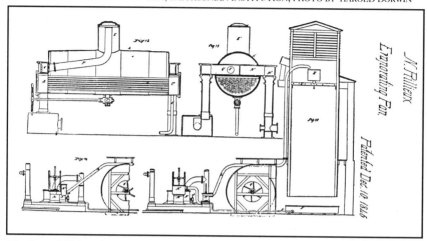

Norbert Rillieux's sugar-evaporating pan revolutionized the sugar-making industry. However, White racial bias denied the inventor his due. None of the chemistry, physics, or technical journals of his time mentioned his work.

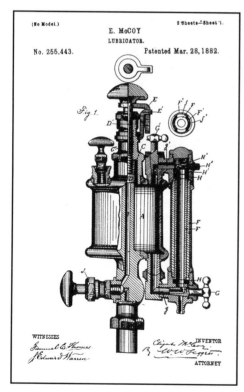

Elijah McCoy's lubricator cup was the cornerstone of his Detroit-based company. Many White companies, upon hearing that the inventor was Black, rescinded their orders for his device despite their need for it. Its incredible capability, though, eventually broke the color barrier and it became standard in the industry.

Although Jan Matzeliger's shoe-lasting machine made Lynn, Massachusetts, America's shoe-making capital, the inventor profited little from his creation.

Prof. Geo. W. Carver, M. Ag.

During the early twentieth century, George Washington Carver was seen as a Black Horatio Alger. His was the era of Babe Ruth, the flappers, the end of Prohibition, and Charles Lindbergh crossing the Atlantic by plane. It was the era of the segregated Negro League, the Harlem Renaissance, jazz, and Langston Hughes.

Benjamin Banneker's African family name was Banneka. The name was subsequently misspelled Banneky in official records before it was given its familiar form. Today, residents of Della, Maryland, are seeking to make the nearby home of the astronomer a national historic park.

Charles Drew resigned his post as director of the American Red Cross in protest of the group's decision to segregate Black and White blood.

smoke. Morgan and his brother Frank were summoned. Using their masks, the two men were able to enter the tunnel when no one else would and rescued a number of men.

For his deeds Morgan became a national hero and was honored by the International Association of Fire Engineers, which made him an honorary member of the Cleveland Citizens' Group. A prominent group of Cleveland citizens presented him with a solid gold diamond-studded medal.

Requests for the mask soon came in from police and fire departments and from mining companies. Morgan found it necessary to employ White salesmen to sell his device in the bigoted Deep South. Often orders from southerners would come in only to be rescinded later, after Whites had learned that the maker of the mask was Black. Morgan's original concept was improved upon and used successfully by the U.S. Army during World War I. The mask soon became standard equipment on the front lines, where troops often encountered poison gas attacks.

THE TRAFFIC SIGNAL

In 1923 Morgan patented his best-known invention. His traffic signal was the precursor to the traffic signals used today. Earlier he had witnessed an accident at an intersection involving a horse carriage and an automobile. The people in the carriage were flung into the street, the driver of the car was knocked unconscious, and the horse had to be shot.

The rules governing behavior at intersections still were evolving. Automobiles were relatively new. Morgan's traffic signal helped revolutionize traffic control and led to the later development of the overhead signal. The signal consisted of a tall pole with a bell on top and two flaps with "stop" printed on them. The flaps were raised and lowered by a hand crank, located near the mechanism's base.

Rather than let racism ruin his ability to market his traffic signal, Morgan sold it to the General Electric Company for forty thousand dollars, a large sum in those days. He followed a path taken by many Blacks in selling his invention to Whites, who in turn profited from it.

MORGAN AND RACE

Morgan never let his success blur his sense of what was happening to other Black people throughout the nation. He served as a treasurer of the Cleveland Association of Colored Men, which later became part of the newly formed National Association for the Advancement of Colored People. His involvement in the NAACP lasted the rest of his life.

During the 1920s he started the Black newspaper the Cleveland *Call,* today known as the Cleveland *Call and Post,* now published in Cincinnati and Columbus as well.

In 1931 Morgan ran unsuccessfully as an independent candidate for Cleveland's city council. "If elected, I will try to lead the people to equal representation," he said during a campaign speech.

His platform included:
1. Relief for the unemployed and a more economic and efficient administration of public affairs
2. Improved housing conditions
3. Better lighting and policing and improved sanitation
4. Improved city-owned hospital accommodations

Though Morgan's bid was unsuccessful, thirty-six years later, Carl Stokes took the oath of office as the city's first Black mayor and the first African American to run a major U.S. city.

In 1943 Morgan developed glaucoma, which robbed him of nearly all his vision. He died on July 27, 1963, in Cleveland after a long illness. He missed by one month the August celebration of the centennial of the emancipation of Africans from the bonds of slavery. He had spoken of his desire to travel to

Chicago for the ceremony. His wife, Mary, ever at his side, died five years later.

Madame C. J. Walker, 1867–1919

Sarah Breedlove McWilliams, known as Madame C. J. Walker, is credited with the development of the modern hot comb. She also is regarded as the first self-made woman millionaire in the United States. Not bad for a woman who started with less than two dollars in her pocket in 1904.

Despite her financial accomplishments, Madame Walker was not the first Black woman to found a Black hair care company. That honor goes to Annie Turnbo Pope Malone, who apparently counted Walker among her employees at one time. However, Walker did revolutionize the Black hair care industry and challenged accepted marketing strategies with her door-to-door approach.

Walker did not invent the first hot comb—reports dating back to the early 1700s credit French Jews with such a device—but there is a debate about who actually first developed the *modern* hot comb. While many say it was Madame C. J. Walker, it was Malone who received the first patent in 1900. Malone's invention was a steel comb—with teeth spaced far enough apart to work on the thick hair of Black women—that could be heated on a stove top.

Sarah Breedlove was born in poverty in 1867 to Minerva and Owen Breedlove on the shores of the Mississippi River. Sarah's parents, both ex-slaves, were sharecroppers who lived on the Burney plantation in Delta, Louisiana.

Sarah grew up in Louisiana cotton fields during the Reconstruction era. And though slavery had ended, the lives of former slaves had changed little. Often they worked long hours under an unforgiving delta sun, hands calloused and bleeding from the spiny cotton plant. They lived in one-room shacks, with no windows, blankets covering the doorways, no indoor toilets, and dirt floors. Sarah's parents both died on the plantation when she was a child.

Life got no better for Sarah after she was taken in at age seven by her older sister, Louvinia. Louvinia's husband physically abused the child and may have influenced Sarah to marry Moses McWilliams in 1881 when she was fourteen. The marriage produced Lelia, who became her mother's constant companion. In 1887, two years after his daughter's birth, Moses was murdered by a White lynch mob.

Vicksburg, Mississippi, before the turn of the century was no place for a Black single mother. Sarah didn't stay long there. Rather, she went north to live with her family in St. Louis. She took on a number of odd jobs, from cook to laundress.

In Walker's day, there was little in the way of hair care for Black women. Many relied on a process of straightening their hair by wrapping and twisting it. It not only was painful but tended to damage hair and make it fall out.

Walker began experimenting with various chemicals— some say she used sulfur—looking for a way to keep her own hair from falling out. She not only halted her hair loss but noted that some had grown back in. She soon began patenting her discoveries and selling them locally.

Walker later recounted in her promotional material the "unusual" dream that led to her hair care invention: "One night I had a dream. . . . A big Black man appeared to me and told me what to mix up for my hair. Some of the remedy was grown in Africa, but I sent for it, put it on my scalp, and in a few weeks my hair was coming in faster than it had ever fallen out." Walker accompanied her "Wonderful Hair Grower" with her development of the metal hot comb.

Following her brother's death in 1905, Walker moved to Denver, Colorado, to live with his widow and four daughters. Soon after, she founded her hair care company. As it grew, she found that she no longer needed to perform domestic work.

Sarah the businesswoman met and married Denver newspaperman C. J. Walker. He was a marketing expert and apparently came up with the door-to-door sales concept that became Sarah's trademark. For a time their union seemed a good one, but C.J. was not comfortable with his wife's growing success, and they soon divorced. Sarah decided to retain his name.

Walker was unable to read or write until well into adulthood. She routinely scribbled her name in such a way that no one could tell she couldn't spell. The act was so successful that when she finally learned to write her own name on a check, the bank would call her up to verify the strange signature.

Perhaps her lack of a good education spurred Madame Walker to push Lelia into college. Lelia attended historically Black Knoxville College in Tennessee. When she graduated, she joined her mother's company. Lelia helped not only with manufacturing the products but also with sales, training, and other aspects of the business. By 1906 she had taken control of the mail-order operation.

In 1908 Madame Walker and her daughter left the "Mile High City" for Pittsburgh, where they founded a beauty school. Lelia College, run by Lelia herself, taught what became known as the Walker Method. Five years later Lelia moved to New York to establish a second Lelia College.

Meanwhile, Madame Walker toured the country, selling her product. She also sold the concept of self-help, particularly among Black women, encouraging them to get into businesses for themselves. By the time she moved her operation to Indianapolis in 1910, she claimed to have more than five thousand sales agents, nearly all of them Black women, earning as much as seven thousand dollars a week. The number of agents grew to more than twenty-five thousand by 1920, Walker claimed.

Madame Walker continued to build her company by hiring key people to mind the business. Freeman B. Hanson, hired to run the Indianapolis operation, met Walker on a train on which he was a porter. He joined Walker's company after finishing law school.

Walker spent the next few years opening beauty parlors in the United States, the Caribbean, and South America.

Her success rested in her ability to exploit a market that had been overlooked by the mainstream. Her methods, however, often drew the wrath of Black leaders who accused her of trying to make Black women look White with her hair straighteners and cosmetics. Many ministers refused to let her address the women in their congregations.

As a Black woman Madame Walker faced the two-headed monster of racism and sexism. In 1912 Walker was snubbed by the educator Booker T. Washington and the National Negro Business League, which refused to let her speak at its convention. But Madame Walker stood up in the middle of the conference and made her voice heard. The following year she was invited back as a guest speaker.

Black women ignored the protestations of the men and rallied around Madame Walker and her business. Soon her success grew to such an extent that she was worth more than one million dollars by 1914. And Madame Walker knew how to flaunt her wealth.

She had a thirty-four-room mansion built on the Hudson River in Irvington, New York, and called it Lewaro, after her daughter (who had married a man named Robinson). The stylish estate became the scene of some of the most opulent gatherings the Black community had seen in this country. Lelia, too, got in on the image-is-everything act, changing her name to A'Lelia.

Walker always remembered where she'd come from, giving away large sums of money to a number of Black organizations. Gifts ranged from five thousand dollars to the Daytona (Florida) Normal and Industrial Institute for Girls, run by educator Mary McLeod Bethune, to five hundred dollars for the restoration of abolitionist Frederick Douglass's home in Washington, D.C.

Then came 1917, the year of the infamous "Red Summer," in which scores of Black men were lynched and otherwise murdered in the cities and on farms by mobs of Whites. That summer was one of the worst on record for lynchings, which were officially overlooked by the government.

Madame Walker joined a group of Black leaders who went to Washington that year to urge President Woodrow Wilson to enact legislation outlawing the lynchings. Wilson would not see them, saying only that he was too busy.

Undaunted, Madame Walker spoke out on the matter as she toured the country, and she encouraged her sales agents to speak out as well. The women sent telegrams to Wilson and other politicos. Eventually antilynching policies were enacted.

Madame Walker's death on May 25, 1919, was mourned throughout the Black community. After a funeral at the mansion, she was buried at Woodlawn Cemetery in the Bronx. For many among the throng of well-wishers who attended the services, she was a vision of what could be and a rejection of all that was negative about African people in this country.

She willed her house to daughter A'Lelia, with the understanding that when she died, she would in turn will it to the NAACP. A'Lelia died during the Depression, and with money hard to come by, the house was sold and the money given to the civil rights organization.

Annie Turnbo Pope Malone, 1869–1957

By the 1920s Annie Malone was worth more than fourteen million dollars. By 1957, however, that amount had dipped to around one hundred thousand dollars.

While Madame C. J. Walker is credited with the development of the modern hot comb, Malone received the first patent for it in 1900.

Malone was not the first Black woman to patent her invention. On July 14, 1885, Sarah E. Goode had patented a fold-

119

ing cabinet bed, the precursor to the Hide-A-Bed. On July 17, 1888, Miriam E. Benjamin had earned a patent for a gong and signal chair, used by U.S. congressmen around the turn of the century to summon their pages.

Annie Minnerva Turnbo was born on August 9, 1869, in Metropolis, Illinois. She was the tenth of eleven children born to Robert and Isabella Cook Turnbo. Not much is known of Malone's childhood. Both parents died when she was very young, and she lived with an older sister in Peoria, Illinois.

Malone took an early interest in hair textures, and during the 1890s she began looking for better hair care methods for Black women. At the time many women were using various combinations of soap, goose fat, and heavy oils, anything to straighten their thick curls, often doing considerable damage to their scalps. Malone experimented, searching for combinations that would diminish the damage.

By the turn of the century Malone had developed a variety of straighteners, oils, and hair growth treatments. While living in Lovejoy, Illinois, she also patented her hot comb, which she dubbed the Wonderful Hair Grower, the same name used by Walker.

PORO

By 1902 Malone had moved to St. Louis, where she and three assistants went door to door, hawking her products. Poro Products—Poro was derived from a West African word that symbolized physical and spiritual growth—was open for business. Malone was a shrewd businesswoman who used the Black press extensively, holding numerous press conferences as she toured the South.

A short-lived marriage to a gentleman named Pope soon followed. She divorced him when he began interfering with her business.

In 1905 Sarah McWilliams, one of Malone's first employees, left St. Louis and headed west to Denver, Colorado. Once there, she married her second husband, took on his name, and began building a company to rival Malone's. The following year Malone trademarked the Poro name and then accused her new rival—Madame C. J. Walker, who had her own Wonderful Hair Grower—of imitating her creations.

Poro College, founded in 1917, was the first center in the United States dedicated to the study and teaching of Black cosmetology. The college was fully equipped with classrooms, barbershops, laboratories, an auditorium, dining halls, an ice-cream parlor, a bakery, a theater, and a roof garden. The facility soon became a social hub for Black St. Louis. The college was a fixture on Poro Corner, complete with an annex and a garage.

Malone employed nearly two hundred people at the college, which preached the merits of a solid public persona, down to the correct walk, talk, and style of dress. By 1926 Malone claimed to have as many as seventy-five thousand Poro sales agents throughout the United States and the Caribbean. During the 1950s and 1960s Berry Gordy, then owner of Detroit's Motown Records, employed a similar strategy in promoting his "Sounds of Young America" image.

The college also served a very public community function. When a tornado ripped through St. Louis in 1927, Poro College was used as a major relief facility for the Red Cross.

MALONE, THE PHILANTHROPIST

In general, the 1920s was a period of expansion and chaos for Malone. With a personal wealth that reached well into the millions, she began to lavish her assets on any charity or cause that came along. She financed the educations of numerous Black collegians, supported several orphanages to the tune of five thousand dollars a year, and gave expensive gifts to employees. She gave Howard University's medical school more than thirty thousand dollars in grants, another five thousand dollars to the St. Louis YWCA, and similar large amounts to several historically Black colleges.

She also made her second husband, Aaron Malone, her chief manager and president. To the public, the Malones were the picture of happiness, the ideal couple. Secretly, however, the two feuded and fought for control of the business.

BEGINNING OF THE END

In 1927 Malone sued his wife for divorce and claimed that he was the driving force behind the company's success and thus deserved half of the business. The divorce proceeding was very messy and very public, dividing many households within the Black community. Such notables as Mary McLeod Bethune, then the president of the National Association of Colored Women, came to Annie Malone's aid in a public show of support. Annie Malone eventually reached a two-hundred-thousand-dollar settlement with her ex-husband and avoided losing her company.

Malone moved her entire operation from St. Louis to Chicago in 1930 and began delegating authority to her numerous managers. She had become a role model to Black women and was much in demand, spending her time on the road at churches, conferences, and conventions.

But with incompetents minding the business in Chicago, Malone was in for another fight to rival the one she'd had with Aaron. A former employee successfully sued her in 1937, claiming credit for some of her products. Another suit filed by a St. Louis newspaper editor so crippled Malone financially that she was forced to sell off various holdings to cover her legal costs.

The federal government also caught up with her in 1943, collecting one hundred thousand dollars in taxes not paid during the 1920s. In 1951 the government received another forty-eight thousand dollars and eventually took control of Poro, selling off most of the property, including the college. Malone died in 1957.

Lloyd Augustus Hall, 1894–1971

"We don't take niggers" came the response from a personnel officer at the Western Electric Company upon seeing Lloyd Hall enter the office seeking a job. Earlier that same person had been so impressed during a phone interview that he offered the recent college graduate a job. But Hall's appearance on Western Electric's doorstep revealed the "mistake" made by the company, which suddenly had no position to offer him.

Dr. Hall was to recover from the slight and become a pioneer in the development of curing salts, which revolutionized the processing and preserving of meats and produce.

SCHOOLING

Hall was born on June 20, 1894, in Elgin, Illinois. His maternal grandmother had reached Illinois from Alabama at age sixteen via the Underground Railroad. His paternal grandfather had been a freedman, who came north to Chicago in 1837 and was one of the founders of the Quinn Chapel African Methodist Episcopal Church, the first and oldest Black church in Chicago. In 1841 the elder Hall became the church's first pastor.

Hall graduated from East Side High School in Aurora, Illinois, as an honor student interested in chemistry. He later said that his love for chemistry began at East. "Chemistry was not well known when I began my high school studies in 1908, but all types of sciences were of great concern to me," said Hall, who was graduated among the top 10 of his class of 125. "During my four years in high school, there were only five Negro-American students—four girls . . . and me." Hall was the captain of his high school debate team, played baseball and football, and ran track. In addition, he made some money delivering newspapers.

The scholarship Hall received to attend Northwestern University was one of four offered him, he said. He continued to work odd jobs while majoring in chemistry. On the road to graduation, Hall met, and for a time teamed with, Carroll L. Griffith, a fellow chemistry student and the founder of Griffith Laboratories in Chicago, where Hall later spent thirty-four years working in food chemistry.

In 1916 Hall earned his degree in pharmaceutical chemistry. He earned graduate degrees at the universities of Chicago and Illinois. After the disappointment at Western Electric, Hall landed a job as a chemist with the Chicago Department of Health. Within a year he was promoted to senior chemist. In 1918 he went to work as chief chemist for the John Morrell Company in Ottumwa, Iowa, a position he held for two years.

From 1917 to 1919 Hall was also appointed chief inspector of powder and explosives in the U.S. Ordnance Department. After the war, on September 23, 1919, Hall and Myrrhene E. Newsome were married. She was a graduate of Western State Teachers College in Macomb, Illinois.

Two years later, as chief chemist for Boyer Chemical Laboratories, Hall began to focus on food chemistry. Of special interest was the problem of preserving meat, which often went bad very quickly. It was not an uncommon practice in those days to season the meat with sugar to make it more palatable.

FINDING THE RIGHT CURE

By 1922 Hall was the president and chemical director of Chicago's Chemical Products Corporation, a consulting lab. One of his clients was his old college chum Carroll Griffith. The two renewed their friendship when Griffith asked Hall to join Griffith Labs. Hall accepted and became Griffith's chief chemist and director of research. He remained with his friend's company until his retirement in 1959.

Before Hall's discoveries, preserving salts and meat-curing products often did not work well. Little was known about them. The use of sodium chloride, or common table salt, as a preservative was standard practice and dated back to ancient times.

Scientists during Hall's time discovered that chemicals containing nitrate—sodium nitrate or potassium nitrate—when added to salt proved efficient in curing the meat, making it redder and more appealing to the eye. Later they found that removing one oxygen atom from nitrate did an even better job. The removal of one oxygen atom from the nitrate produced nitrite. Its combination with the hemoglobin in the meat resulted in the red coloring and made the meat last longer.

Hall concluded, however, that both nitrate and nitrite still worked too slowly to be effective in preparing the meat for the curing salt. By the time salt penetrated the meat, it already had rotted. Hall devised a method of enclosing nitrate and nitrite inside the salt crystal, thus preserving the meat much more quickly and enhancing its freshness.

Hall's process, known as flash-drying, involved quickly drying the mixture of the three chemicals by cooking them over a high heat. The new substance had the appearance of salt, and its use ensured the preservation of the meat before it was cured.

However, his breakthrough led to other concerns, particularly in regard to the storage of the salt mixture. When stored in containers, the mixture absorbed water from the air and clumped into a solid mass, limiting its effectiveness. Hall returned to the lab in search of chemicals that could absorb the moisture away from the salt, known as hygroscopic agents. His experiments produced a combination of such an agent—glycerine—and alkali metal tartrate. This new combination, added to the original salt mixture during flash-drying, produced crystals that were more powdery in substance and less likely to cake. By chemically softening the water before flash-drying, Hall further refined his product.

In addition to developing a new meat-preserving process, Hall developed sterilization techniques for foods and spices. Many food packers seasoned their meats with cloves, cinnamon, ginger, paprika, allspice, sage, onion powder, and garlic powder before shipping. The thinking at that time was that these spices preserved meat. The thinking was wrong. The meat often rotted more quickly, making it almost impossible to ship.

Hall discovered that these spices contained bacteria in the spores of molds and yeasts. By using ethylene oxide gas in a vacuum chamber with certain foods, Hall found a way to enhance the appearance of the product and reduce spoilage. He developed seasonings, emulsions, bakery products, antioxidants, and protein products. (Hall's sterilization method still is utilized throughout the world by hospitals for such items as bandages, dressing, drugs, sutures, and cosmetics.)

A final hurdle in preserving food was to retard the spoiling of fats and oils. Hall developed an antioxidant, which counteracted the air's effect on the fats, which kept them from becoming rancid as quickly as they had previously.

A FOOD EXPERT

During World War II Hall's services were again enlisted. He was a member of the committee on food research of the scientific advisory board for the Quartermaster Corps of the U.S. Army. His methods were used in preserving foodstuffs for the military.

After the war Hall served on the state food commission of the Illinois Department of Agriculture (1944–1949). From 1946 to 1948 he was a consultant to the George Washington Carver Foundation. From 1948 to 1955 he served on the Food Technology Council of the Illinois Institute of Technology.

In 1951 Hall was involved in patenting a process that reduced the time needed for curing bacon from one to two weeks to mere hours. Hall's other areas of interest included detergents, vitamins, and asphalt.

Also in 1951 Hall began a four-year term on the executive board of the Institute of Food Technologists, of which he had been a charter member in 1939. He served as editor of the organization's magazine, *The Vitalizer*, in 1948. In 1961 he spent six months in Indonesia as a consultant to the United Nations Food and Agricultural Organization.

Hall's appointments, honors, and board seats were numerous. In 1954 he became chairman of the Chicago chapter of the American Institute of Chemists. The following year he was named to the organization's national board of directors, the first African American to hold such a position there. He served on the institute's committee on professional education. The Chicago chapter awarded him an Honor Scroll in 1956 for his achievements in food chemistry. The institute gave him another honorary membership award in 1959.

Other honors and memberships came from the American Association for the Advancement of Science, the American Public Health Association, the New York Academy of Sciences, Phi Tau Sigma (an honorary food science fraternity), the Chicago Conference on Brotherhood, the Chicago Committee of 100, the Hyde Park-Kenwood Conservation Community Council, and the Chicago Planetarium Society. From 1962 to 1964 Hall, an appointee of President John F. Kennedy, served on the American Food for Peace Council.

Hall also had been an outspoken advocate for civil rights. From 1932 to 1934 he sat on the executive committee of the Chicago chapter of the NAACP, and he was on the board of the Chicago Urban League from 1935 to 1936.

When Hall retired from Griffith Labs, he moved to Pasadena, California, where he spent the remainder of his life. He published more than fifty papers and acquired some 105 patents in the United States and abroad. Hall died in 1971.

Ernest Everett Just, 1883–1940

Ernest Everett Just pioneered the study of cell life and human metabolism and explored egg fertilization. In the 1920s and 1930s he was the first to unlock secrets of cell function, shattering many long-held scientific theories about cell structure and function. During his day Just was regarded as one of the leading experts on egg cells and the development of marine animals.

Just was the first to challenge popular scientific thinking on the essential elements of life. He focused on the material both around the outer edge of the cell and just inside the cell membrane, known as the ectoplasm of the cell. Biologists of his day ignored the ectoplasm, turning their attention solely on the cell's nucleus. Just eventually proved that the outside region of a cell was crucial in cell and egg development.

"[Ectoplasm] is keyed to the outside world as no other part of the cell," he said. "It stands guard over the peculiar form of the living substance, is buffer against the attacks of surroundings and the means of communication with it."

Scientists still are far from knowing all there is to know about embryonic development, even with the advent of electron microscopes and the discovery of biochemical cycles, protein sequences, and double helixes. But Just saw the key role played by the cell surface in the development of the whole cell as being as important to the life of the cell as was the function of the nucleus.

THE SON OF A TEACHER

Just was born on August 14, 1883, in Charleston, South Carolina, to a middle-class family. His father was a dock worker who died when his son was four. His mother was a teacher and responsible for most of his early education. To help make ends meet, Just had to go to work as a farmhand at a young age.

He attended an all-Black high school in Orangeburg, South Carolina. When he finished at age seventeen, his mother sent him north for more schooling. He spent his first summer away from South Carolina working in New York, and used the money to pay his way into the Kimball Academy in New Hampshire, a four-year boys' prep school.

Just's education in the South had done little to prepare him academically. At Kimball he was placed in the lowest class, where he essentially repeated four years of high school. In three years he finished the secondary requirements and was graduated from Kimball as valedictorian.

With the help of loans and scholarships, Just attended nearby Dartmouth College in 1903. Though the college may have been the first American institution to admit Blacks—as early as 1770, according to university records—Just's presence on campus was unusual but apparently uneventful.

His experiences during the first two years at Dartmouth were not unlike those of other students, apparently to his dismay. In the early part of this century Dartmouth was a football power, and the rivalry with the much-hated Harvard University crimson was on the minds of all who wore the Dartmouth green. Just later spoke of feelings of disappointment with what he saw as a university less interested in academic success than in athletic crowns.

A biology course changed all that. There he found the intellectual stimulation he sought. Just began his work in cytology, the study of cells. In his junior year Just was elected to the Phi Beta Kappa Society. Acclaimed as a classicist, a journalist, and a poet, he stood first in the Dartmouth graduating class of 1907 at the age of twenty-three. He was the only magna cum laude of his year, a dual biology and history major with a flair for research.

Just left Dartmouth that same year to teach at Howard University in Washington, D.C. In 1912 he was named head of

Howard's biology department, a position he held until his death. At Howard his study of the nature of living cells began to draw notice in the community of biologists.

Just had set his mind on the natural sciences, although medicine was the easier path to a career for Blacks of that day. This created a long-running conflict with his duties as an instructor at Howard. His expertise in biological research techniques became so much in demand that it cost him heavily in time for his own research. Howard University was no place for research; without financial support, he was heavily burdened with teaching duties.

WOODS HOLE

From 1909 to 1930 Just spent every summer but one studying marine biology at the Marine Biological Laboratory under the auspices of the University of Chicago, in Woods Hole, Massachusetts, located on Cape Cod. His first studies were with invertebrates. Many of the great biologists from around the world have spent at least some time at the Woods Hole facility. Many more have studied under one of those who have done research there.

Biologic research at Woods Hole was regarded highly in the scientific community around the turn of the century and remains vitally important today. Many scientists saw oceans as the beginning of animal life on this planet. Marine life offered scientists many new avenues for research on protoplasm, the human body's insides, and the eggs of sea creatures could be cultivated, dissected, and experimented on in a number of ways.

The Woods Hole of Just's day also was a research haven for A. H. Sturtevant, T. H. Morgan, and Calvin Bridges, American giants in chromosome genetics; K. S. Cole and Selig Hecht, the American pioneers of biochemical and biophysical neurology; and the noted cytologist E. B. Wilson.

In 1909 Just studied as a research assistant under the University of Chicago's Dr. Frank Rattray Lillie, a noted marine biologist of the day and the director of Woods Hole. During the summers of 1911 and 1912 Just assisted Lillie in the study of the fertilization and breeding habits of sea urchins and sandworms.

Lillie, whom Just regarded as his dearest friend, later wrote about his colleague and the twenty summer sessions spent in Massachusetts: "He learned to handle the material with skill and understanding. In consequence, he was in great demand, especially by physiologists who knew their physics and chemistry better than biology, for advice and assistance which he rendered generously."

SPINGARN MEDAL

The inaugural year of the NAACP's awarding of the Spingarn Medal, given to "the man or woman of African descent and American citizenship who shall have made the highest achievement ... in any honorable field of human endeavor," was 1915. Just was the award's first recipient, and though he accepted the honor, he was somewhat embarrassed by the attention.

Upon hearing that he had been chosen to receive the award, the thirty-two-year-old Just at first wrote to the civil rights organization to object to his selection. "My contributions have been meager," he wrote. "It rather upsets me to learn that I am expected to be present at the award ceremony, doubtless in the presence of a large audience. I feel deeply that I ought not court publicity."

Just was not fond of crowds. He also had little time for small talk. For hours at a time he and other scientists worked together in the lab, competing to see who could say the least. One evening a professor proudly announced that he had beaten Just that day. He had spoken only three words. Just quickly

131

corrected his colleague, saying with a smile, "Oh, no, I beat him today. I said only one."

The following year, 1916, Just earned a doctorate in zoology—magna cum laude—from the University of Chicago. That same year he completed his sixth paper based on the work he had done at Woods Hole.

STUDY OF MARINE LIFE

For more than twenty years Just studied and experimented at Woods Hole with the reproductive cells of marine animals. In his writings Just said that understanding the workings of cells would be useful in finding cures for such dreaded diseases as sickle-cell anemia, cancer, leukemia, and other diseases caused by abnormal cell growth.

He also found something of a home for himself at the Massachusetts laboratory and a place to pursue serious study. Often he was the first one to arrive each summer, as much as three weeks ahead of the others, and was the last to leave as fall approached.

He studied the early development of the eggs of marine invertebrates—sea worms, starfish, and sea urchins—at Woods Hole until he left there for good in 1930. For a decade Just was Lillie's gifted young collaborator. But by the end of World War I he had built his own reputation, notably for his knowledge of and control over the handling of marine eggs and sperm at Woods Hole.

He knew the effects of temperature on his subjects. He understood the importance of careful experimental controls and came up with ways to handle living cells without damaging them.

Many of Just's contemporaries acknowledged the scientist's ability to take unusual and imaginative chances with his experiments. This often led him into areas of study that were revisited years later. During his work with eggs, he applied varied amounts of magnetic energy to them to determine the effects on cell division; he found a notable difference. Scientists looking to the stars in the 1960s used some of his methods by sending biosatellites into orbit; they wished to study the effects of the earth's magnetism and radiation on an assortment of plants and animals that were on board.

It was said that Just got to Woods Hole early to ensure that the marine animals he was to use for his experiments were in the best possible shape. He particularly showed concern over the manner in which the animals were captured because he believed it had a bearing on his findings. He pioneered ways of collecting egg and sperm cells and methods for studying them.

Just's insistence on the gentle capture of marine animals was crucial to his work with the eggs of the sea creatures. Many eggs lasted only about a day outside the mother, even under the best conditions, making utmost care a necessity. Given the short life span of the eggs, Just had to conduct his microscope observations and experiments into the early hours of the morning.

The collection of sandworm eggs, for example, required a certain amount of patience. Just noted that the worms hatched near the laboratory and swarmed together as the moon was between three-quarters and completely full. He found that by using a lamp to simulate moonlight, he could entice the worms out of hiding and gather the samples he needed.

Eventually Just devised a method of separating male and female worms and controlling fertilization. By snipping off the male and female sex organs, he could release the egg and sperm cells into a clean saltwater environment and, with the use of his microscope, study the most minute details of reproduction.

Just soon came to be regarded as the foremost expert on the egg development of sea life. Much of his acclaim was based on his insistence that he work only with healthy eggs. Only then, he said, could he be absolutely certain that the changes he observed were accurate. "An experiment should never in the least way be clouded by uncertainty concerning the normal process," he said.

JUST AND LOEB

At Woods Hole Just met the University of Chicago's Jacques Loeb, a weighty figure in behavior, physiology, and public debate. Loeb at first befriended Just and was an ardent supporter of the NAACP and W.E.B. Du Bois. But when Just found errors in some of Loeb's conclusions, the friendship ended, resulting in a hateful letter written by Loeb to the Rockefeller Institute for Medical Research in 1923. The letter succeeded in ending Just's chances for an appointment to the institute. Just's presentation created a rift between the pro- and anti-Loeb forces and placed him at the center of the controversy.

Loeb's angry 1923 letter may have been a key factor in Rockefeller's rejection of Just. A research position at the Rockefeller Institute might have been "symbolic for the whole Black race," according to a recent biography on Just. Loeb, still stinging from having some of his theories disproved by Just, wrote that he had tried to "help and encourage" Just but concluded "the man is limited in intelligence, ignorant, incompetent, and conceited."

Around the beginning of the century Loeb had devised what became known as the lysin theory of fertilization. It stated that two substances were needed for artificial, or lab-induced, parthenogenesis. (The term "parthenogenesis" refers to an egg that develops without the aid of sperm.)

Loeb claimed that if the egg were treated with butyric acid, then seawater with a higher-than-normal salt concentration (hypertonic salt water) were applied, the egg would develop into its larval stage, making it able to swim. Loeb also claimed that adding the substances in reverse order would bring about the same effect. The theory was universally accepted.

By 1922 Just disproved Loeb's theory by demonstrating that the hypertonic salt water alone was effective in inducing the growth of an unfertilized egg.

Despite his discoveries, Just never was invited to do research at many of the nation's other great labs. A wealth of temporary research grants did not ease the pain of being rejected as a full-time faculty member by every major university in the United States.

A GROWING RESENTMENT

By 1930 Just had received numerous awards and was recognized worldwide. As a member of the corporation of the Marine Biological Laboratory, he was on the editorial board of the *Biological Bulletin*, Woods Hole's official journal. He also had been named vice-president of the American Society of Zoologists.

But Just had become embittered over never being asked to study at the prestigious institutions. He later said that because of the racial discrimination he faced, he steered many of his students away from following in his footsteps. Instead he advised them to become doctors, so that they would find greater opportunities.

The effects of racial bigotry stretched as far as the Howard campus, which was unable to offer Just the type of facilities needed for his work as the result of the lack of financial support that plagued all historically Black colleges. Just never blamed the university. In fact, he understood.

In 1928, after years of indecision, the Julius Rosenwald Fund finally agreed to support Just's department at Howard, for books, equipment, and research, over the next five years. No other Black in science had ever had such support. Despite the grant, the damage to Just's psyche already had been done. The remainder of his life saw him slip farther into bitterness over the conditions facing Blacks and the frustration of wondering how his work would have been received had he been White.

Also in 1928, Just made his first visit to Europe, where he spent six months at a zoological station on the Bay of Naples. He recalled later that everyone was kind and his research went well. One of the women scientists, apparently taken by his charm and looks, dubbed him Black Apollo.

Just returned from Europe as a fan of the zoological station, going so far as to try raising funds for an American zoological station. In the early 1930s he returned to Europe as a guest professor at the Kaiser Wilhelm Institute for Biology in Germany. He also studied at the Sorbonne in Paris.

AN UNGRACEFUL END

In the summer of 1930 Just paid a surprise visit to Woods Hole. The occasion was Lillie's sixtieth birthday and fortieth year in Massachusetts. Just was the last of five former Lillie students to speak. At the conclusion of his dry and technical talk Just looked over the crowd and said, "I have received more in the way of fraternity and assistance in my one year at the Kaiser Wilhelm Institute than in all my other years at Woods Hole put together."

The room fell silent. Just never ventured to Woods Hole again.

Wrote an apparently understanding Lillie:

> When [Just] withdrew from Woods Hole to work in European laboratories, his loss to the scientific community was deeply felt. An element of tragedy ran through all Just's scientific career due to limitations imposed by being a Negro in America, to which he could make no psychological adjustment in spite of earnest efforts on his part. In Europe, he was received with universal kindness and made to feel at home in every way; he did not experience social dis-

crimination on account of his race, and that contributed greatly to his happiness there. That a man of his ability, scientific devotion, and of such strong personal loyalties as he gave and received, should have been warped in the land of his birth must remain a matter of regret.

The Great Depression and the death of Julius Rosenwald marked the end of Just's Howard grant in 1933. It also marked a dramatic change in his personal life. Just had fallen in love with a young German philosophy student named Hedwig in the summer of 1931. He made seven trips to Europe to see her. Even his wife of many years and their children in Washington began to fade from his life as he rejected anything that reminded him of America.

By 1936 Just had cut nearly all ties with family, friends, and country. That year, from his new home on the blue Bay of Naples, he wrote a letter to Italian dictator Benito Mussolini: "As an American negro who for more than 25 years has contributed to the progress of biological science without having attained a place . . . which such service deserves, I desire earnestly the opportunity to continue my labors in Italy and thereby cooperate [as] your energetic leadership accelerates Italy to a magnificent destiny." The dictator never responded.

From 1938 to 1940 Just and Hedwig, nearly broke, lived together in France. At that time his books were about to appear in the United States. In the first, *The Biology of the Cell Surface*, published in 1939, he theorized that the surface of a cell (or cell membrane) was as important to life as the nucleus. In his second book, *Basic Methods for Experiments on Eggs of Marine Animals*, also published in 1939, he detailed his scientific process. The two books capped a career in which he had published more than fifty papers on cell biology between 1912 and 1937.

Then the world fell in. France fell to the invading Third Reich. All foreigners were forced to leave the country. Just had no choice but to return to the country he had once vowed never to see again. Hedwig, pregnant and now Just's wife by virtue of a Riga divorce, accompanied him. Ill and unhappy, he returned to teaching at Howard.

Just died shortly after returning to Washington, of cancer of the pancreas at age fifty-seven on October 27, 1940.

In 1957 the Woods Hole scientists released a revised version of Just's second book, *Basic Methods for Experiments on Eggs of Marine Animals.*

Charles Richard Drew, 1904–1950

Dr. Charles Richard Drew was the first person to develop the blood bank. His introduction of a system for the storing of blood plasma revolutionized the medical profession. Drew first utilized his system on the battlefields of Europe and the Pacific during World War II. He later organized the world's first blood bank project—Blood for Britain. He also established the American Red Cross Blood Bank, of which he was the first director.

Drew was born on June 3, 1904, in Washington, D.C. He was the eldest of five children. At Dunbar High School he starred in track, football, baseball, and swimming. He was graduated in 1922. Drew graduated in 1926 from Amherst College in Massachusetts, where he received the Messman Trophy, given to the student who has brought the most honor to the institution. He was captain of the track team and a halfback on the college's football team. Drew spent the next two years as a biology and chemistry instructor and the director of athletics at Morgan State University in Baltimore, Maryland.

DEVELOPMENT OF PLASMA STORAGE

In 1928 Drew enrolled at McGill University in Montreal, Canada, where he studied medicine. He became known for his athletic prowess there as well, winning championships in the

138

low hurdles, high jump, and broad jump. He also saw a man's life saved via a blood transfusion, he later recalled, and the incident triggered his interest in blood and plasma preservation.

In 1933 Drew earned his Master of Surgery and Doctor of Medicine degrees from McGill and served a medical internship at the Royal Victoria Hospital in Montreal.

At that time the Canadian medical community was working on more effective ways to make use of the relatively new blood-typing system, first discovered in 1901 by Viennese pathologist Karl Landsteiner. The four types—A, B, AB, and O—were discovered to be distinct. The researchers found that in whole-blood transfusions, the blood groups must be compatible. If not, the red blood cells rupture and clump together, a condition that can cause jaundice, kidney damage, and death. Only type O blood can be universally given, while only people with type AB blood can receive any other blood type.

Blood transfusions, though risky in Drew's day, were not new. As early as the fifteenth century, the Incas of Peru were known to perform transfusions. In 1667 French physician Jean-Baptiste Denis pumped lamb's blood into his human patients.

As a young doctor Drew saw many of his patients die from the absence of a suitable blood donor. In one particular case, Drew allowed his own blood to be used to save a life.

In 1935 Drew became a resident in surgery and taught pathology at Freedmen's Hospital at Howard University in Washington, D.C. There he devised a way to separate plasma from whole blood, making the blood easier to store and paving the way for the creation of the first blood banks.

Prior to this discovery, the rapid breakdown of red blood cells had prevented the storage of blood for more than one or two days. When red blood cells break down, potassium is released into the liquid portion of the blood, the plasma, thus spoiling it. At the same time Drew was conducting his research, doctors in Chicago, also looking for ways to retard spoilage, had tried freezing whole blood, but to no avail.

Drew also found that blood that was handled roughly or knocked around tended to break down quickly. Borrowing a page from the Chicago effort, he began to experiment on the blood of animals, refrigerating and separating the red blood and the yellowish plasma in separate containers, recombining them during transfusion. He settled originally on two weeks, then on one week as the ideal amount of time the blood could remain fresh.

Then Drew made his most important discovery. He found that it was not always necessary to recombine the red blood with plasma. He found that in cases in which whole blood was not needed for transfusion, the plasma sufficed. Further, he found that without red blood in the plasma, there was no need for blood-typing, for pure plasma could be administered to anyone.

PRESBYTERIAN BLOOD BANK

In 1938 Drew was offered a fellowship in blood research at New York City's Columbia Presbyterian Hospital. That same year he convinced the hospital to establish its first blood bank. In 1940 he earned his Doctor of Science degree—the first African American to hold such a degree—from Columbia University. There he wrote a dissertation on "banked blood" and developed a technique for the long-term preservation of blood plasma.

In the first four months of its blood bank Presbyterian administered more than four hundred transfusions, and more than eighteen hundred between 1938 and 1940.

His reputation spread to Britain, where he was asked to set up that country's first blood bank. During earlier research he had learned that dried plasma was easier to transport, so he arranged for a large shipment of dried plasma to be sent overseas.

140

In 1939 Drew married Minnie Lenore Robbins, an economics professor at historically Black Spelman College in Atlanta. Lenore was a native of Philadelphia and a graduate of State Teacher's College in Cheyney, Pennsylvania, a historically Black institution. She had received her bachelor's degree from Columbia University's Teachers College and a master's degree in home economics education from Cornell University. Drew and his wife had met in Washington and got to know each other while she was serving on the Spelman faculty from 1935 to 1939. After their wedding Lenore joined her husband in New York, where she assisted him in his research. The couple moved to Washington in the early 1940s and had four children: daughters Charlene, Bebe, and Sylvia and son, Charles junior.

In 1941 Drew was appointed director of the American Red Cross blood donor project. He was the first Black to hold the post. But even his presence was not enough to battle bigoted views that Black blood was somehow tainted and not fit for Whites. The government decided that the armed forces would not mix Black blood with that of Whites.

The edict from the U.S. War Department read: "For reasons not biologically convincing but which are commonly recognized as psychologically important in America, it is not deemed advisable to collect and mix Caucasian and Negro blood indiscriminately for later administration to the military forces."

Drew responded angrily, calling a press conference at which he blasted the edict and pointed out that there was no scientific evidence to indicate differences in blood by race. Said Drew: "The blood of individuals may differ by blood groupings, but there is absolutely no scientific basis to indicate any difference in human blood from race to race."

As a result of the controversy, Drew resigned his Red Cross post in 1941—the same year he was appointed—and returned to Howard as head of the department of surgery, chief surgeon, chief of staff, and medical director at Freedmen's Hospital.

The practice of segregating blood continued in Red Cross blood banks for many years after Drew stepped down. The doctor continued to speak out against racism and White supremacy the remainder of his life.

THE MYTH SURROUNDING DREW'S DEATH

Drew died on April 1, 1950, following an automobile accident in North Carolina while he was on his way to a medical conference at Tuskegee Institute. In the car with him were several young Black doctors. He was forty-six.

There are conflicting stories on the exact cause of Drew's death. Most popular accounts claimed that he had died because White hospitals had denied the Black doctor the very process he had pioneered—a blood transfusion. Later accounts of Drew's death do not support this theory. Noted Black scholars have argued that Drew's condition was beyond hope and that efforts to give him blood were made.

Perhaps the story came from the death in 1937 of jazz singer Bessie Smith, who was said to have been turned away from a White hospital and allowed to bleed to death following an auto accident. But this also did not happen. Those closely involved with the Smith tragedy later said that by the time help could reach her, one of the jazz singer's arms was nearly severed and she was close to death. *The Death of Bessie Smith*, a 1960 play by Edward Albee, further popularized the myth.

These stories live on in popular culture. In some ways, ways that historians may never fully appreciate, the idea that it could have happened stands as a symbolic reminder of the devaluation of Black achievement by an ungrateful nation. Asked once what she thought of the circumstances surrounding her father's death, Drew's daughter Charlene Drew Jarvis, now a Washington, D.C., politician, said that while she believed every effort had been made to save her famous father, many more Blacks were turned away from White hospitals and left to their own devices.

In April 1986 a six-foot granite and bronze marker was dedicated on Interstate 85 in Alamance County, between Greensboro and Durham, marking the spot where Drew's car spun out of control.

After her husband died, Lenore reared their four children, stayed active in the Washington community, and returned to teaching. All the children finished college, and three have advanced degrees. Lenore wrote articles on her husband's life and accomplishments, including one for *Reader's Digest,* and lectured extensively on his life at schools and health facilities across the country.

M. Lenore Drew was eighty when she died at her home in Columbia, Maryland. She had Alzheimer's disease.

Louis Tompkins Wright, 1891–1952

In 1915 Louis Tompkins Wright was a medical student at Harvard University in Massachusetts when he first heard of filmmaker D. W. Griffith and his newly released movie *Birth of a Nation,* which depicted Reconstruction-era Blacks as clowns and savage brutes. Enraged by the film's racist and anti-Black themes, Wright halted his studies for three weeks to protest its showing in a Boston theater. Despite his professional accomplishments at the time, and in times to come, Wright never lost sight of the realities of the world around him.

Wright was regarded by many as a pioneer in the field of clinical antibiotic research. He was the first physician to explore intradermal (under the skin) smallpox vaccinations, to create a brace for patients with head and neck injuries, and to use chlortetracycline—a yellow, crystalline antibiotic in the tetracycline family—on humans.

143

A FAMILY OF EDUCATORS

Born in La Grange, Georgia, on July 23, 1891, Wright received his entire education, from elementary school to college, in the world that was Clark University in Atlanta.

Wright's father, Dr. Ceah Ketcham Wright, graduated in 1881 from Meharry Medical College in Nashville, Tennessee. The elder Wright died when Louis was four, leaving Lula Wright with very little money with which to support her two sons. She took a job as a matron in the women's dormitory at Clark.

Young Louis was about to enter elementary school when his mother began working at Clark. The historically Black college was in the midst of its own cultural revolution. Scores of students from New England had migrated to the South to teach in religious and other schools.

Dr. William Fletcher Penn, who in 1898 was the first Black man to earn a degree from Yale University, came to teach at Clark. Lula Wright married Penn when Louis was eight years old. Penn played a key role in shaping the future doctor's life and became a mentor for Wright in his pursuit of medicine.

Wright was graduated as class valedictorian from Clark in 1911, then applied to the medical school at Harvard University. He was told by Dean Otto Folin that he could enter if he passed a chemistry examination. According to Wright, he returned home and studied for two days before returning to take the test, which he easily passed.

THE BATTLE BEGINS

At first Wright was informed that he would not be allowed, as a student in obstetrics, to perform deliveries of White babies at Boston's Lying-In Hospital, where all Harvard medical students were trained. He fought the ruling, arguing that he had paid his tuition and was entitled to the same advantages afforded to any other student. Wright's protest led to the abolition of the university's "separate but equal" practices and allowed him to continue his studies unhindered.

Wright spent his summers working as a field hand back in Georgia to earn the money to continue his schooling. In 1915 he was graduated cum laude and fourth in his class.

Despite his credentials as a Harvard doctor, gaining respect from bigoted Whites in the North or in the Deep South was slow in coming. Massachusetts General Hospital and Peter Brent Hospital, both in Boston, refused to offer Wright internships because of his race, so Wright followed in the footsteps of many Black doctors, scholars, and scientists of his day and went to Howard University in Washington, D.C.

The battle for respect continued in the nation's capital. While interning at Howard's Freedmen's Hospital, Wright had a run-in with a U.S. senator who insisted on addressing Wright as Sam, a nickname of disrespect used by Whites to keep Blacks "in their places." After a severe scolding from Wright, the politician unsuccessfully tried to have him removed from the hospital.

Wright also wrote a paper at Howard arguing that the Schick test, administered to patients to determine whether they were susceptible to diphtheria, was a valid test for African Americans. Many regard the major work as the first such originated at the hospital.

After completing his internship in 1916, Wright passed medical examinations in New York, Maryland, and Georgia. He returned home to Atlanta to begin his practice and found unchanged the racial hatred he had left behind. When he went to register his medical license, the White clerk, apparently unimpressed with Wright's credentials, refused to address the doctor by his last name. This was a common practice of southern Whites, who did not consider Blacks worthy of such respect.

Wright insisted that he be referred to as "Dr. Wright."

The clerk responded with more venom, asking a question that never would have been posed to a White doctor and in a tone designed to reduce Wright to his "place" in southern society. "Have you been peddling any dope or abortions?" came the sarcastic inquiry.

Wright stood, faced down his antagonist, and replied, "Let me tell you something. I will choke you right here if you open your Goddamned mouth again!" Wright had no further trouble procuring his license.

WAR DOCTOR

With the entry of the United States into World War I Wright enlisted in the U.S. Army Medical Corps as a first lieutenant. There he introduced an intradermal method of vaccinating for smallpox that the Army soon adopted. By injecting the saline-diluted vaccine into the skin, rather than the vein, of the patient, Wright eliminated some of the side effects associated with the drug.

Wright later was sent to France, where he became the youngest surgeon placed in charge of a base hospital. Many white officers, including his own colonel, regarded his brash manner as annoying. According to historians, the colonel sent Wright to the front lines, secretly in the hopes that the doctor would be killed by a "lucky" German bullet. Though he was gassed, he avoided the gunfire and returned to base. Awarded the Purple Heart and discharged with the rank of captain, Wright soon rose to the rank of lieutenant colonel in the Medical Reserve Corps.

Wright returned home from the war and married Corinne Cooke on May 18, 1918. The couple moved to New York, where he opened a surgical practice. The following year he was appointed clinical assistant visiting surgeon at White Harlem Hospital. Four White doctors resigned in protest over the hiring of the hospital's first Black doctor. His post became permanent a year later. He remained there for most of his career.

Jane Cook Wright, who carried on her father's work later in life, was born in 1919. Sister Barbara, who also became a physician, was born the following year.

NEW YORK

In 1928 Wright was appointed police surgeon for New York City, the first Black in that post. Two years later a group of New York physicians interested in racial justice formed the Manhattan Medical Society with Wright as its leader. The group opposed a plan by the Rosenwald Fund to open segregated Black hospitals in the city. The society also turned down grants from Rosenwald to build segregated medical schools for Blacks.

Wright also was a prominent activist within the National Association for the Advancement of Colored People as a member of the national board. Through the NAACP he established a national medical committee to expose cases of racial discrimination. He blasted popular statements of the day that claimed that Blacks had more syphilis, tuberculosis, and cancer than Whites and the implications that this somehow proved genetic inferiority. He pointed out that these health problems were due to a lack of adequate medical care, and he called for real reforms in medical care for African Americans. Today the lack of adequate care remains a serious concern in poor Black neighborhoods.

In 1934 Wright was the second Black admitted to fellowship with the American College of Surgeons. (Dr. Daniel Hale Williams, who had been a charter member in 1913, had been the first.)

SURGEON AND SPECIALIST

Wright's specialty was head and neck surgery. To ease the recovery of his patients, he devised a special neck brace for

147

neck fractures that is used today. Considered among the leading experts on head injuries, he was asked to write a chapter on the subject in the eleventh edition of Charles Scudder's *Treatment of Fractures* in 1938. He also invented a special surgical blade to be used in working on fractures on and around the knee.

In 1939 the American Board of Surgery recognized him with the title "diplomate," a physician who has been certified as a specialist by a board of professionals in his or her field. That same year, as a result of having been gassed in the war, he developed pulmonary tuberculosis and was confined to a bed for three years. He still managed to remain busy, doing some research and speaking out on social ills. In 1940 he was awarded the NAACP's Spingarn Medal for his medical successes and his battle against discrimination.

In 1943 Wright was named director of surgery at Harlem Hospital. Five years later he became president of the hospital's medical board.

Myra Adele Logan was an intern and a resident under Wright at Harlem Hospital. Logan later distinguished herself as the first woman to operate on a human heart and the first Black woman surgeon to be a fellow of the American College of Surgeons.

At Harlem Hospital Wright had turned his attention to the study of lymphogranuloma venereum, a sexually transmitted viral disease that wrecks the body completely, leaving its victim an invalid.

An East Indian doctor named Subberow, an associate of Wright's during his days at Howard, discovered a new antibiotic called Aureomycin and gave a sample to Wright to test on his patients. Wright became the first person to administer the drug experimentally on humans in 1948, with positive results. Between 1948 and 1952 he wrote more than thirty papers on the topic and eight more on Terramycin, another drug used in the treatment of venereal disease.

Wright entered the field of cancer research in 1948. In all

he published fifteen papers on his work on the effects of various drugs and hormones on the cancer cells. By this time his daughter Dr. Jane Wright was working with him; she eventually continued researching on her own.

The John A. Andrews Memorial Hospital at Alabama's Tuskegee Institute awarded Wright a citation in April 1952 for his work on multiracial health programs nationwide. That same month he was guest of honor at a dinner in New York, attended, among others, by Dr. Ralph Bunche, the U.S. representative to the United Nations, and former First Lady Eleanor Roosevelt.

Wright suffered a fatal heart attack on October 8, 1952. In 1969 Harlem's new hospital was named in his honor.

"Louis was not like today's specialists," wrote his wife, Corinne, after his death. "He was a man who could think in many areas. His mind was so versatile about the whole human being that he could go into any area and find something creative to solve that problem."

Frederick McKinley Jones, 1892–1961

Frederick McKinley Jones invented the first automatic refrigeration system for trucks. His cooling system later was adapted for use on ships and railway cars.

Jones was born in Cincinnati, Ohio, in 1892. His mother died when he was nine, and he managed to complete only the sixth grade. He was raised by a priest in Covington, Kentucky, until he was sixteen.

When he left the rectory, Jones took on a number of odd jobs, from pinboy at a bowling alley to a mechanic's helper at a Cincinnati garage. Within three years his skills and love for cars had netted him a promotion to shop foreman. By nineteen he had also built and driven several cars in racing exhibitions. Often he raced his company's cars without permission—for which he was fired.

Later Hall took a chief mechanic's position on a thirty-thousand-acre farm near Hallock, Minnesota. He continued reading about cars and applied his knowledge whenever possible.

During World War I Jones was a sergeant in the U.S. Army and served in France as an electrician. After the war Jones returned to Minnesota. He started to study electronics, eventually building a transmitter for a new Hallock radio station.

Joseph Numero, who owned a motion picture equipment company, hired Jones as an electrical engineer. Numero's company made sound equipment that was used in movie houses throughout the Midwest.

Jones gained local fame for taking silent-movie projectors and converting them to talking projectors, using various odds and ends. In 1939 Jones invented, and received a patent for, a ticket-dispensing machine for movie houses.

Jones and Numero eventually formed a partnership called the U.S. Thermo Control Company, with Jones as vice-president.

By the 1930s Jones had devoted his time to making portable air-cooling units for cross-country trucks that could keep food and other perishables cold. A need for a unit for storing blood serum for transfusions and medicines during World War II led Jones into refrigeration research. A version of those refrigeration systems is still in use today. In 1944 Jones was elected a member of the American Society of Refrigeration Engineers.

U.S. Thermo eventually became a multimillion-dollar operation by making refrigeration systems for trucks, trains, ships, and planes. During the 1950s Jones was a consultant to the U.S. Department of Defense and the U.S. Bureau of Standards.

Jones had more than sixty patents, with forty in the area of refrigeration.

He died in Minneapolis in 1961.

Richard B. Spikes, ?–1962

Spikes designed the directional turn signal on the 1910 Pierce-Arrow automobile. He also held a patent for the automatic gearshift (December 1932).

Other patents include a modern version of the railroad semaphore in 1906, a beer keg tap for the Milwaukee Brewing Company in 1910, an automatic "car washer," and what he called a "fail-safe" braking system for buses in 1962.

David Baker, 1881–?

David Baker's inventions included an elevator scale that safeguarded against overcrowding. He also shares credit with Professor T. V. Baquet of New Orleans for the creation of what he called a "sanitary" cuspidor.

Born in Louisville, Kentucky, on April 2, 1881, Baker eventually wound up in New Orleans. There he spent ten years in charge of elevator service at the Board of Trade Building. For a time he also worked as a streetcar transom operator.

Records indicate that he took classes at the Media Night School in New Orleans and correspondence courses from the National Correspondence School, Washington, D.C.

THE MODERN ERA

Percy Julian, 1899–1975

Nicknamed the soybean chemist, Percy Julian is best known for his discovery of a way to synthesize large amounts of cortisone, used in treating rheumatoid arthritis, from soybean oil. He also synthesized the drug physostigmine, used to treat glaucoma. He is known as well for inventing a weatherproof coating for battleships.

The grandson of former slaves, Julian was born on April 11, 1899, in Montgomery, Alabama. He was the eldest of six children—along with James, Emerson, Mattie, Irma, and Elizabeth—born to James Sumner Julian, a railway mail clerk, and Elizabeth Lena Adams Julian, a schoolteacher. His two brothers went on to become doctors, while all the sisters earned master's degrees.

Julian's grandfather Cabe was a sharecropper and a slave before that. He had lost two fingers when his slave captors discovered that he could write; for such an offense, this was considered proper punishment in virtually all slave states.

Percy Julian grew up around the turn of the century in racially segregated Deep South, where many of those old master-slave traditions remained alive. In later years he recalled walking on many a hot summer day behind his grandfather through the Alabama fields, tending crops. Julian always credited his elders as the motivating force behind his achievements.

A CHANCE TO LEARN

Julian always said his lifelong dream was to practice chemistry. As a boy he'd go up to the window of the White Montgomery high school and peer in at the White children in the chemistry class. A White policeman would chase him away from the segregated building.

Julian attended the private Normal School for Negroes in Montgomery. After being graduated in 1916, he enrolled at De Pauw University in Greencastle, Indiana. Because of his inadequate high school education, he was admitted to De Pauw as a "subfreshman" and took high school courses along with his college work.

But the circumstances of his enrollment at De Pauw were less important to Percy Julian than the fact that he was there. He was fulfilling a wish that had appeared years earlier in the mind of his grandmother Lavonia, an ex-slave. With the help of her son James, Percy's father, Lavonia earned money by selling produce at Montgomery's Monroe Street open-air market.

One day Joan Stuart, a teacher at the Normal School, convinced Lavonia that James had the ability to go beyond sixth grade, which was all that was required of Black youngsters. James's mother used some of the money she earned on Monroe Street to pay his tuition into the high school, with the goal of eventually enrolling him at De Pauw, not far from Stuart's hometown of Danville, Indiana.

Although James never made it to De Pauw, his son did,

154

eventually being graduated in 1920 as class valedictorian and as a member of the Phi Beta Kappa and Sigma Xi honor societies.

DE PAUW AND THE JULIANS

While at De Pauw, Julian befriended Kenneth Hogate, later the editor of the *Wall Street Journal,* whose father knew Joan Stuart from her days in Indiana. Kenneth, a member of Sigma Xχ, arranged for Julian to live in the fraternity house in exchange for work as a waiter.

As the only Black student on the Greencastle campus, Julian had few social options. On weekends he either spent time with local Black families or went to nearby Indianapolis and the Senate Avenue YMCA. The Y became his haven. He could shoot pool, play the piano, and prepare himself for the week ahead.

As Julian was nearing the end of his schooling at De Pauw, his parents moved the family north to Putnam County, Indiana. One by one, the Julian youngsters were graduated from Greencastle High School and followed their older brother to De Pauw.

Percy's brother James enrolled in 1920, the year Percy was graduated. James later transferred to the University of Chicago. He was the only Julian sibling not graduated from what became the family institution, though he was granted an honorary Bachelor of Arts degree in 1970 at age sixty-eight. Sisters Mattie, Irma, and Elizabeth became teachers and business executives.

SNUBBED

As De Pauw's top chemistry student Julian expected to receive offers from some of the top graduate schools. Those offers were not forthcoming. In a 1969 biography Julian recollected his disappointment at being refused admission to White graduate schools because of his skin color.

"I stood by as day by day my fellow students in chemistry

155

came by saying 'I am going to Illinois'; 'I am going to Ohio State'; 'I am going to Michigan'; 'I am going to Yale.' 'Where are you going?' " he recalled.

After a conversation with Professor William Blanchard, his academic adviser, Julian learned why there had been a delay. White deans from the nation's top White schools had told Blanchard that "the bright colored lad" would have trouble finding work in his field after college or that his presence would be disruptive. It was suggested that Whites would refuse to take lessons from him, refuse to work with him, or try to sabotage his work. They advised Julian to seek a teaching post at a historically Black school, where a doctorate was not needed.

"There went my dreams and hopes of four years," Julian remembered. "As I pressed my lips to hold back the tears, I remembered my breeding, braced myself, and thanked [Blanchard] for thinking of me."

Taking the advice, Julian left De Pauw to teach chemistry at historically Black Fisk University in Nashville, Tennessee. Then, in 1922 he was awarded a fellowship at Harvard University, where he earned a master's degree in chemistry the following year.

Again his race had been a factor, for he was refused an assistantship because the administrators feared that White students would be offended at the thought of having to obey a Black instructor. Instead he was offered a series of what were referred to as minor fellowships until he left in 1926 for then all-Black West Virginia College for Negroes (now the predominantly White West Virginia State University).

Julian was not satisfied at being the college's one-man chemistry department and left West Virginia College within a year to take a post as associate professor and director of the chemistry department at Howard University. Mordecai Johnson, who had become Howard's first Black president in 1926, made a mission of recruiting Black faculty and hoped to send them on to nearby Catholic University to earn their doctorates.

Catholic refused them all, including Julian, on the basis of their race.

SOYBEAN SYNTHESIS

In 1929 Julian finally received a fellowship from the General Education Board—an organization promoting Black education—to study for his Ph.D. in organic chemistry at the University of Vienna, Austria, with Dr. Ernst Späth. Späth had successfully synthesized nicotine, found commonly in tobacco, and created artificial ephedrine, useful in the treatment of respiratory illnesses.

Julian developed an interest in the soybean, which had been used by scientists in Europe in the creation of certain drugs. (Among these was physostigmine, which causes the pupil of the eye to contract.)

He also became interested in processes by which soybeans were used in the synthesis of sex hormones, which led to the creation of birth control pills. Prior to the emergence of artificial hormones, their only reliable sources were the small amounts of cholesterol in the brains and spinal cords of cattle and soybeans.

Julian, who earned his doctorate in 1931, returned to Howard as a full professor and with two assistants who had studied with him in Austria. But after a disagreement with zoologist Ernest E. Just over whether a White chemist should be allowed to teach at Howard (Just was opposed), Julian resigned in 1932 and accepted an invitation to return to De Pauw from Blanchard, his old professor, who had become a dean. Back at De Pauw, Julian and Dr. Josef Pikl—a colleague in Vienna and at Howard—continued learning how to make synthetic physostigmine, a potent treatment for glaucoma. The drug, in its original form, had been discovered in 1865 by two European scientists as a by-product of Calabar beans, the seeds of the physostigma plant. The drug relieves the pressure on the eye caused by glaucoma, thus reducing damage to the retina.

A BREAKTHROUGH

By 1934 Julian's research had become widely known. Nonetheless, his work nearly was halted when the university decided to discontinue its financial support. Finally an outside grant was secured and the work resumed.

At the time of Julian's discoveries many considered Oxford University Professor Robert Robinson the leading chemist in the field of physostigmine synthesis. His conclusions differed greatly from Julian's, leaving many in the scientific community to doubt the value of the latter's research.

But in February 1935 Julian, Pikl, and Blanchard proved Robinson's methods wrong by successfully completing their own synthetic process. Accolades poured in from across the United States, France, Japan, Switzerland, and other parts of the globe. Julian had done what once had seemed impossible.

Later that year Julian married Dr. Anna Johnson, a sociologist and a trustee at MacMurray College in Jacksonville, Illinois, who had earned her doctorate from the University of Pennsylvania. The couple had a daughter and a foster son, both of whom went on to professional careers.

REJECTION

Despite his fame, Julian could not land a permanent teaching post. Blanchard's recommendation of Julian as the first Black to chair De Pauw's chemistry department was refused by university officials who feared faculty reaction.

Julian then applied for a tenure-track post at the University of Minnesota but was refused. He was offered a post with the Appleton-based Institute of Paper Chemistry, but a local statute against "housing" Blacks overnight in the Wisconsin town ended that discussion.

He finally was offered a job in 1936 by W. J. O'Brien of the Chicago-based Glidden Company, a manufacturer of paints, varnishes, and food products. Julian accepted a position as chief chemist and director of research. At Glidden he developed a process to use soybean protein to coat and size paper, to size textiles, and in cold-water paints. The process replaced the comparatively expensive practice of using casein, a milk protein, to coat paper.

Julian's Aero-Foam, another soybean derivative, was used by American servicemen in World War II as a smothering agent to put out gasoline and oil fires. It was affectionately referred to by the troops as bean soup.

He also completed the work he had begun in Austria on the creation of substitutes for the male and female hormones. They since have been used to treat cancer, to protect unborn babies, and to prolong male virility.

In 1947 he was awarded the NAACP's Spingarn Medal, for the highest achievement made that year by an African American. Two years later he received the Distinguished Service Award from the Phi Beta Kappa Society.

JIM CROW

Julian's triumphs still didn't impress racist Whites. On Thanksgiving Day 1950, his new home in the White Chicago suburb of Oak Park was attacked by racist White arsonists. No one was injured, and the house was not seriously damaged.

A Chicago *Sun* editorial on November 23, 1950, blasted the would-be arsonists: "We wonder if these cowards . . . would refuse to use the lifesaving discoveries of Dr. Julian because they came from the hand and brain of a Negro. No! The bigots welcome the discoveries of Dr. Julian the scientist, but they try to exclude Dr. Julian the human being."

Less than a year later a firebomb was thrown from a speeding car at the Julians' house, while he and his wife were in Baltimore attending his father's funeral. Seven-year-old Faith and eleven-year-old Percy, Jr., both in the house, were not harmed. That same summer Julian was notified that an invitation to speak at a national meeting of scientists at Chicago's Union League Club had been rescinded because of a club policy prohibiting Blacks.

In 1967 Julian joined Asa T. Spaulding, president of the Black-owned North Carolina Mutual Life Insurance Company, to form a coalition of some forty-seven wealthy Blacks to raise one million dollars to finance civil rights lawsuits brought by the NAACP.

In 1970 he wrote: "How much can a human being be expected to endure? Even today, I marvel that the greatest majority of intellectuals did not become hopeless psychotics."

Julian's home was under constant guard for a year following the threats to his and his family's lives.

JULIAN LABS

Julian left Glidden in 1954 and established Julian Laboratories near Chicago and Laboratorios Julian de Mexico in Mexico City and in Guatemala. In the Mexico City labs Julian discovered that yams worked as well as, if not better than, soybeans for synthesizing his synthetic products.

He also created a synthetic version of cortisone, or cortexolone, from the soybean. Cortisone was hailed as a wonder drug and used in treating arthritis. The drug had been discovered at the Mayo Clinic and was made from the bile of oxen, which unfortunately produced very small amounts of the drug. Julian's synthetic drug corrected this inadequacy.

In 1956 Julian became the first African American, and the first layperson, to head the Council for Social Action of the Congregational Christian Churches. He was active in Chicago civic affairs, held the post of vice-president on the board of trustees of Dr. Daniel Hale Williams's Provident Hospital—where Williams performed the world's first successful open-heart operation—and served on the boards of directors of the local Urban League and Roosevelt College.

In 1961 he sold his Chicago company for $2.3 million to the Smith, Kline and French pharmaceutical company but retained his post as president. He also sold his Guatemala operation to the Upjohn Company.

RIGHTS AND HONORS

Julian received numerous awards and nineteen honorary degrees, published more than two hundred papers, and held more than eighty chemical patents. During his lifetime he urged Black scholars to use science as a means of breaking down "a philosophy of defeatism" and giving hope to all.

Julian received honorary doctorates from De Pauw in 1947, Fisk University (1947), West Virginia State College (1948), Morgan State College (1950), Howard University (1951), Northwestern University (1951), and Lincoln University in Pennsylvania (1953).

He died on April 19, 1975, of liver cancer at St. Theresa's Hospital in Waukegan, Illinois.

The following year Anna Johnson Julian donated $51,000 to De Pauw in her husband's name. The money went toward the establishment of the Julian Memorial Chemistry Fund and the Julian Memorial Scholarship Fund. In 1980 De Pauw's $7.2 million science building, opened in 1972, was renamed in Julian's honor.

Ironically, days after Julian's death a resolution mourning his death was passed by the Alabama House of Representatives and signed by Governor George C. Wallace. In 1963 it was Wallace who, standing on the steps of the University of Alabama, declared, "I draw the line in the dust and toss down the gauntlet before the feet of tyranny and I say 'segregation now, segregation tomorrow, and segregation forever.' "

Samuel L. Kountz, 1930–1981

Samuel L. Kountz helped develop the prototype for a machine that could preserve kidneys for up to fifty hours after being removed from a donor's body—valuable in transplant procedures. The Belzer kidney transfusion machine was named in honor of Kountz's partner, Dr. Folkert O. Belzer.

In 1964, working with transplant pioneer Dr. Roy Cohn, Kountz became the first person to transplant a kidney from a mother to her daughter. It was the first time that a kidney had been successfully transplanted between other than identical twins.

Kountz also developed a technique for detecting and treating the rejection of a transplanted kidney by its new host body. Prior to his breakthroughs, only 5 percent of kidney transplant patients could expect to live more than two years after their operations. Today the chances of survival are greatly increased.

Kountz was born in Lexa, Arkansas, in 1930. According to the legends told about him, Kountz, the son of a Baptist minister, was eight years old when he decided that medicine would be his life.

Having failed his entrance exam to Arkansas A&M College, Kountz went directly to the school's president to plead his case. The administrator, impressed by the plea, admitted Kountz, making him the first African American student at the college. He was graduated third in his class in 1952.

Kountz later earned his master's degree from the University of Arkansas, and at the insistence of Senator J. W. Fulbright—whom Kountz had met while attending Arkansas A&M—he enrolled in and was graduated from the University of Arkansas Medical School. He was the school's first Black graduate.

TRANSPLANT RESEARCH

It took Kountz three years of experimenting with dogs in the United States and Great Britain to develop many of his theories on kidney transplants. Kountz believed that primates would become a chief source of transplanted organs because theirs were more readily available than human organs. Recently surgeons in Pittsburgh, Pennsylvania, tested his theory, successfully transplanting a kidney from a baboon into a human. The patient lived for a short time.

Through his research he learned that certain cells in the body would attack the small blood vessels of the alien kidney, which eventually would die from lack of oxygen. Kountz discovered that large doses of methylprednisolone could retard the rejection of a transplanted kidney. For years the drug was standard in managing kidney transplants.

In 1964 Kountz and Cohn made their historic transplant of a kidney from a mother to her daughter.

In the late 1960s, at the University of California, San Francisco, Kountz created one of the country's largest kidney research facilities. In 1967 his research team developed a prototype machine that could preserve a kidney outside the body for up to fifty hours.

Kountz was given the Investigator Award from the American College of Cardiology, and he was awarded an honorary law degree from the University of Arkansas in 1973.

During his life Kountz performed more than five hundred kidney transplants, including one live on the NBC *Today* program in the mid-1950s, while he was surgeon in chief at Kings County Hospital in Brooklyn, New York.

Kountz died in 1981, after coming down with an undiagnosed brain illness during a visit to South Africa in 1977.

Ralph Gardner, 1922–

Ralph Gardner's methods of interpreting catalytic chemical reactions led to advances in the chemical, petrochemical, pharmaceutical, and polymer and plastics industries. To put it simply, his work led to the development of hard plastics. It also opened the door to developing practical solutions to such problems as pollution and hazardous waste disposal. He also worked on the Manhattan Project to develop an atomic bomb.

Gardner was born on December 3, 1922, in Cleveland, Ohio. Both his parents were college graduates. His father was a pharmacist who earned his degree from the University of Buffalo, and his mother earned her degree from the University of Illinois.

When he was in the eighth grade, his parents bought him a magic set. It was fun, he later recalled, but not quite what he had in mind. The following year he got a chemistry set. He decided then on a direction for his life.

Gardner began college at the Case School of Applied Science in 1939 but soon grew disillusioned with the treatment afforded him. He was enrolled in a cooperative program designed to find work for its students. The only Black in the program, he was told that efforts to secure him a job in the hospital kitchen or as a busboy had been fruitless.

In anger, he transferred to the University of California, Berkeley, for a year. He then came back to the Midwest and his mother's alma mater, the University of Illinois. He was graduated as a chemistry major in 1943 and moved to Chicago.

ATOMIC SCIENTIST

Gardner took a research post at the University of Chicago's Argonne National Laboratories, where he spent the next four and a half years on the classified plutonium research that was known as the Manhattan Project—the making of the atomic bombs that were dropped on Japan in 1945. Gardner worked under Italian-born nuclear scientist Dr. Enrico Fermi and radioactivity scientist Dr. Nathan Sugarman.

Gardner was one of more than a dozen Black scientists who were involved in research on the atomic project. The Black scientists known to be involved in the metallurgical laboratories also included Lloyd Albert Quarterman, Edward A. Russell, Moddie Taylor, Harold Delaney, Benjamin Scott, J. Ernest Wilkins, and Jaspar Jeffries. A second group at Columbia University included George Dewitt Turner, Cecil Goldsburg White, Sydney Oliver Thompson, William Jacob Knox, and George Warren Reid, Jr.

Despite his work on the atomic bomb, Gardner could not find an academic job in his field when he left Argonne in 1947.

Earl D. Shaw, 1937–

Fighting the little battles has been a life's work for physicist Earl D. Shaw. He is one of only a handful of African American physicists and the inventor of a state-of-the-art free electron laser used in the study of chemical reactions, biological functions, and the electronic properties of semiconductors. With more than forty publications to his credit, Shaw is regarded as one of the world's preeminent physicists.

In 1991 the Mississippi native "retired" to his post as a professor at Rutgers University in order to pursue his two great loves: physics and teaching. "What I want to do is study molecular and biological systems," said Shaw, who is doing just that at Rutgers after years with AT&T Bell Laboratories in New Jersey. "What I'm really interested in is looking at the DNA in the human body."

A SERIES OF ACCIDENTS

Looking back, Shaw said a series of what he called accidents led him into the sciences. He was born in 1937 and lived on the Hopson plantation near Clarksdale, Mississippi. And though his mother had not finished elementary school, she taught her son to read. He remembered his earliest formal education coming near the Clarksdale, Mississippi, fields, where his parents worked, and later at a nearby three-room schoolhouse.

It was the dream of Shaw's father to provide a way out of the fields for his family. Like many poor southern Black men, he went north, to Chicago, to find work with the hope of later sending for his family. "The lady next door to us in Chicago knew me from the fields of Mississippi," Shaw recalled.

When Earl was twelve, tragedy struck. His father had been murdered in the city on the shores of Lake Michigan. It was not long after that Earl's mother packed them both up and moved to Chicago as well, fulfilling the elder Shaw's hopes.

"My grandfather was fiery," said Alan Shaw, Earl's son, recalling the stories his father and grandmother told. "When he died, the family lost a sense of what to do. Chicago represented something negative from the beginning."

The Shaws were not alone in their move to the North. As was the case with earlier Black migrations from the South, whole families were uprooted in search of better lives and new identities, as many families fled their sharecropper status on what once were slave plantations.

CHICAGO

In many ways Shaw's memories of Chicago parallel scenes of street life in the 1990s. Back then the Blackstone Rangers and other youth gangs ruled the avenue. "They weren't shooting each other, but they were beating each other with chains. I'm sure I got a better education then than is available now," he said, thinking about today's gang violence.

Alan Shaw recalled his father's telling him stories about growing up in Chicago, of striving to stay one step ahead of trouble. Perhaps it was that desire to escape the life and death he saw around him that drew him into physics, Alan mused. "He went into disciplines that were the farthest from the streets," he said.

When Earl Shaw first enrolled in Crane Technical High School at age twelve, the school was roughly three-quarters White, he recalled. When he left four years later, Blacks outnumbered Whites by that same margin. "I went in at a time when racial boundaries were moving," he said.

In 1954 a White friend from high school talked Shaw into attending the University of Illinois. "If it hadn't been for that White kid, I might not have gone to college," he recalled with fondness.

He went on to get his master's degree in physics from Dartmouth College in 1964. After earning his doctorate from the University of California at Berkeley, he signed on as an adjunct professor of physics at Howard University in Washington, D.C., through the mid-1970s.

LASER SCIENTIST

The continued development of laser technology plays a part in more than human medical research. Until 1978, for example, physicists had no control over the amount of energy emitted by electrons. Then a group of Stanford University scientists developed a method for speeding up and slowing down electron movement by freeing up an electron from its nucleus. The resulting light energy was translated into a range of ultraviolet (blue) or infrared (red) levels.

"If you want to study anything, you want to be able to change it," said Shaw, who took the original free electron laser concept and developed his unique version, which is used in several hospitals and in radiation therapy for cancer patients. "The free electron laser allows for much higher energy in the future than we now have. My laser allows me to tune the wavelength by turning a knob. That has been very hard to do."

Bell physicist and former colleague Walter P. Lowe said that Shaw's accelerator—which runs the laser—works in much the same manner as a radio tuner, picking up "signals" from across the spectrum. The difference between Shaw's device and those previous, Lowe argued, is in its range. "If your radio could only work at three places, you could only hear three stations. With his, you could look at areas of the spectrum that have never been heard," said Lowe.

Shaw's son, Alan, who received his doctorate in physics from the Massachusetts Institute of Technology, said he has retraced his father's footsteps many times on his own life journey. "He is a pioneer in the Black community," said Alan Shaw. "He is one of the Black geniuses who are not written about."

When Earl Shaw earned his doctorate in 1969 from the University of California at Berkeley, laser research was his passion. "I knew the field was underdeveloped, so I kept looking for new ideas. When I was in grad school, I built a lot of equipment," he said.

BELL LABS

When he arrived at Bell Labs in the mid-1970s as a researcher, Shaw was the first African American hired to do research. Eventually, thanks to Shaw's insistence, other noted Black physicists would follow, including Shirley Jackson, Roosevelt Peoples, Kenneth Evans, and Walter P. Lowe.

Lowe said he owes much of his own success as a scientist to Shaw and the example he set; "I could not imagine such a thing as a Black scientific community evolving the way it has without some involvement from him. He stands among the top people in the scientific community in terms of accomplishments and respect."

According to Lowe, Shaw's demeanor with those around him flies in the face of the stereotypic image of unreachable genius. "When you talk of genius," he said, "you talk of some-one who's aloof or vague or someone you can't get close to. He's not like that. We can walk down the hall and he'll intro-duce me to the president of the company and then introduce me to the lady who cleans the floors and have the same rapport with both."

"There's now a history of Blacks in research at Bell Labs," said Shaw. "But our progress certainly is not exponential."

Michael Croslin, 1933–

In a 1980 interview, inventor and businessman Michael Croslin, most noted for his invention of a computerized blood pressure device called the Medtek 410, described his inventive process: "People ask how do you become an inventor. There is no such thing. You have to have something going for you to being with. I don't know what it was for me in my youth, except that I always liked to dabble around with machines.

"If you sit in your living room and look around, your eyes will probably fall on a dozen things that can be improved or redesigned. You have to ask yourself what it is you want to do and then put down on paper, no matter how nonsensical, all the steps it would take.

"It may take a week or a year or five years, and it will take a lot of money but the rewards are fantastic."

Produced by the Medtek Corporation—a biomedical company he founded in 1978—the Medtek 410 was slightly larger than a calculator and relied on blood motion to determine blood pressure rather than the sound of pumping blood as was the case with traditional devices. Previously readings from a blood pressure apparatus—called the sphygmomanometer—could be flawed because of outside noises, humidity, and the doctor's hearing, vision, and judgment. Croslin's device gave a reading in a matter of seconds, displaying the blood pressure and pulse on a digitized screen.

"The old blood pressure device left a lot to be desired," Croslin said in an interview. "The doctor had to watch a falling column of mercury and listen through a stethoscope. All the doctor's senses were involved—eyesight, hearing, the noises going on around him, and his condition or feelings at the time."

In all, Croslin produced more than forty patents, including a thermometer that reads body temperature in less than five seconds; a refractometer, which measures sugar levels and protein content in urine; and an intravenous pump, which measures out exact dosages of prescribed drugs.

All the devices belong to the Medtek Corporation, a New York-based firm, founded and mostly owned by Croslin, which develops and manufactures electronic diagnostic medical equipment. The Medtek 410, which took Croslin nearly twenty years to finish, has been the mainstay of the company.

Croslin was born in 1933 in Frederiksted, St. Croix, U.S. Virgin Islands. Abandoned by his parents as an infant, he was taken in and reared by a local family, who named him Miguel Britto.

In 1945 the twelve-year-old Croslin ran away. Later he said he left tropical St. Croix to escape the waiter, bartender, or beach bum existence that awaited him. Borrowing money from friends and strangers, he purchased a ticket to the United States.

After a brief period in Georgia working odd jobs and attending a Jesuit school, Croslin headed north to Wisconsin, where he was taken in by a family who adopted him and gave him their name—Croslin. He finished high school at fourteen and three years later was graduated from the University of Wisconsin with a Bachelor of Science degree. In 1950 he joined the U.S. Air Force, which trained him as a pilot. Among the last Blacks trained in an all-Black squadron prior to the integration of the military, he served in both Korea and Vietnam.

After the Korean War he settled in New York, where he was taken in by a Brooklyn family. He attended New York

University and received a Bachelor of Science degree in mechanical engineering in 1958. He later returned to NYU and earned a master's degree in electrical engineering in 1963 and a doctorate in biomedical engineering in 1968. During that time he also picked up a master's degree in business administration from Columbia University.

After graduation in 1958, Croslin was hired by the Pall Corporation in Glen Cove, New York. Croslin recalled that David Pall, owner of the engineering firm, was the only person who would hire him. Pall also encouraged Croslin to go into business for himself, as he did in 1960.

With about two hundred dollars saved and with loans from friends and the Small Business Administration, Croslin opened a one-room operation he called the Dungeon. Short on funds, he sold off one of his patents to Grumman Aircraft for fourteen thousand dollars. He sold a number of his early patents to make ends meet, he recalled.

Croslin later founded International Applied Science Laboratory, Inc., a research and development firm that lasted nearly a decade. By 1970 the company's sales had reached more than two million dollars. The following year, however, the business went bankrupt. Croslin blamed the demise on his business partner, to whom he had entrusted financial control.

Ironically, during his company's early years the emerging Black Panther party picketed Croslin, claiming that he did not hire Blacks.

In 1978 Croslin founded the short-lived Medtek Corporation. At first business was good. In the first year, for example, the forty-person operation grossed more than $3 million, then $8 million the following year. But by 1981 the company reported sales of $750,000 and losses of more than $1 million. In 1982 he sold the company to Quest Medical, Inc., of Carrollton, Texas, and severed all ties with Medtek the following year.

Today Croslin operates a consulting firm in New York.

His clients include NASA, Corning Incorporated, IBM, and American Hospital Supply.

Paul Brown

In 1968 San Franciscan Paul Brown invented a toy that swept the country called the Wiz-z-zer, a stringless spinning top sold by the toymaker Mattel. More than fifteen million tops were sold between 1968 and 1978, when they were discontinued.

The Wiz-z-zer concept was very simple. A jagged plastic strip was inserted into a hole in the top. When the strip was yanked out, the top spun. Several "spin-off" products, including a set of toy race cars, followed Brown's invention.

Born in Springfield, Ohio, Brown worked for the Army Corps of Engineers as an assistant chief for technical services. A few fat royalty checks later he resigned and moved with his wife, Louisa—a former school principal—to Redwood City, California.

In all, Brown has tallied more than sixty inventions. Success did not come easily. Fourteen companies said no to his invention before he knocked on Mattel's door.

George R. Carruthers, 1940–

George R. Carruthers was one of the two scientists who developed the lunar surface ultraviolet camera and spectrograph used on the moon by *Apollo 16* in 1972. He was the instruments designer; William Conway, another scientist, adapted it for the mission.

Carruthers was born in Chicago in 1940 and reared on the city's South Side. At the age of ten, he made his own telescope. He went to Chicago's Englewood High School.

He earned his doctorate from the University of Illinois, Chicago, in 1964 at the age of twenty-four, then joined the

Rocket-Astronomy Program at the Naval Research Laboratories in Washington, D.C., where he still works. There he worked on a design for an electromagnet imaging device. He invented his camera-spectrograph in 1972, when he was thirty-two. It became the earth's first moon-based observatory.

The device was used to gather photographic images of the earth's upper atmosphere, and it was the first human-made instrument to detect the existence of hydrogen deep in space. The device later was adapted for use on *Skylab 4*, which tracked the progress of the Kohoutek comet in 1974.

Christian C. L. Reeburg

On August 14, 1978, Christian C. L. Reeburg of Jamaica, New York, received a patent for his invention, the grease gun stand. The stand allows a person to operate a grease gun with one hand, leaving the other hand free to manipulate the area to which the grease is applied. Prior to this invention, both hands were needed to hold the gun cylinder and operate the trigger.

Richard L. Saxton

Richard L. Saxton of Indianapolis picked up a patent on February 6, 1981, for his invention of a sanitary tissue dispenser for a pay telephone booth.

William C. Curtis, 1914–1976

Dr. William Curtis was a key contributor to the development of radar technology. Among his creations are the Black Cat weapons system, the MG-3 fire control system, the 300-A weapon radar system, and the Airborne Interceptor Data Link—all of which were employed by the U.S. military as part of its cold war arsenal.

A graduate of Tuskegee Institute, Curtis spent twenty-three years with the Radio Corporation of America. He was Tuskegee's first dean of engineering and mentor to the famed Tuskegee Airmen.

Otis Boykin, 1920–1983

Boykin invented the control unit for the cardiac pace-maker. His device, a flat wirelike resistor, controls the amount and rate of current flowing to the heart. The resistor also has been used in missiles, radios, televisions, computers, and space-ships as well as in burglarproof cash registers and chemical air filters. All told, Boykin is credited with more than twenty-five electrical devices.

Born in Dallas, he attended both Fisk University and the Illinois Institute of Technology in 1946 and 1947. Ironically, he died of heart failure in Chicago in 1983.

Katherine C. G. Johnson, 1918–

Johnson was instrumental in NASA's Flight Dynamics and Control Division. She assisted and led in the development of practical systems for tracking spacecraft. It was her job to know exactly where the Apollo astronauts were during every moment of their moon missions in the late 1960s and early 1970s.

O. S. "Ozzie" Williams, 1921–

Williams is credited with inventing the first airborne radar beacon, used to locate downed planes. He also was chief developer of the Apollo lunar lander's guidance engines.

He attended New York University's College of Engineering, where he earned his bachelor's and master's degrees.

Williams's services as a design engineer were employed

by Republic Aviation, Greer Hydraulics, and the Thiokol Chemical Corporation. As vice-president of Grumman International he journeyed to West Africa in 1973 to establish a foreign headquarters.

Herman Russell Branson, 1914–

Herman Branson is noted for his research on the structures of proteins. Working together with Nobel-prizewinning chemist Dr. Linus Pauling, he helped identify the alpha and gamma helical structures of proteins. This breakthrough was critical in understanding how proteins—nature's building blocks—function.

Branson was born on August 14, 1914, in Pocahontas, Virginia. He was class valedictorian in Dunbar High School in Washington, D.C., then attended the University of Pittsburgh before transferring to Virginia State College, where he finished summa cum laude. He earned his doctorate in physics from the University of Cincinnati in 1939.

His work took him into the area of sickle-cell anemia research. He has published more than seventy-five articles and been awarded honorary science doctorates from Pennsylvania's Lincoln University, Virginia State College, and the University of Cincinnati.

Branson was the third president of historically Black Central State University of Ohio and spent fifteen years as president of Lincoln University, stepping down in 1985.

James E. Millington, 1930–

In 1964 Millington invented an electrical insulating paper that could be used in transformers and regulators for the Allis-Chalmers Company. For his effort, he was awarded five thousand dollars.

Born on March 13, 1930, in New York, Millington earned

175

his undergraduate degree from Lincoln University of Pennsylvania in 1951. Two years later he added a master's degree from the University of Western Ontario. He earned his doctorate in chemistry at Western Ontario in 1956.

Robert Bundy, 1912–

Bundy developed a basic design for a portable radar device that was used in World War II by Allied troops during the Normandy invasion. He also is credited with the creation of an X-ray system for airplanes that detects weapons and small wires.

W. Lincoln Hawkins, 1911–

At Bell Laboratories in Murray Hill, New Jersey, Hawkins was one of a team of scientists who developed a weatherproof underground cable. Prior to the breakthrough, cables were dug up and replaced every five years because of damage.

Hawkins is credited with fourteen patents involving the protection of plastics from oxidation.

Alfred A. Bishop, 1924–

Alfred Bishop holds a patent for a flow distributor, used on nuclear reactor cores.

Born on May 10, 1924, in Philadelphia, Bishop earned his bachelor's degree from the University of Pennsylvania (1950). Soon after, he joined the Philadelphia Naval Experimental Station as a chemical engineer. He worked in the same capacity with the Fischer and Porter Company of Hatharo, Pennsylvania. He added a master's degree in chemical engineering from the University of Pittsburgh to his list of credentials in 1965 and a doctorate in mechanical engineering from Carnegie-Mellon University in 1974.

Joseph Blair, 1904–?

The Augusta, Georgia, native holds patents for a type of speedboat (1942) and for an aerial torpedo for long-range bombing that he developed in 1944. That patent was not accepted until 1958.

Philip Gamalieh Hubbard, 1921–

Hubbard invented the water "anemometer," used to measure water turbulence. His instrument was based on the original wind anemometer, invented in 1805 by Royal Navy Admiral Francis Beaufort.

Born on March 4, 1921, in Macon, Missouri, Hubbard earned his bachelor's degree in electrical engineering (1946), his master's in mechanics (1949), and his doctorate in mechanics and hydrology (1954) from the University of Iowa.

Arnold Hamilton Maloney, 1888–1955

Arnold Hamilton Maloney, the nation's first Black professor of pharmacology, discovered that the drug picrotoxin was effective in treating victims of barbiturate poisoning.

Born on July 4, 1888, Maloney earned his bachelor's degree from Naparima College in 1909. He received his master's from Columbia University in 1910 and his M.D. from Indiana University in 1929. Two years later he earned a doctorate in pharmacology from the University of Wisconsin.

As head of Howard University's pharmacology department during the 1930s, Maloney published more than twenty articles in the United States and Belgium.

The inventions of Robert A. Pelham, Jr. (1859–1943), included a pasting machine, a tabulator that was used in the census count of manufacturers, and a tallying machine that was used to count populations. Born January 4, 1859, Pelham worked for the Detroit *Free Press* from 1884 to 1891.

Born May 10, 1868, in Lexington, Kentucky, Shelby Davidson is credited with inventing a mechanical tabulator that may have been a forerunner of the modern adding machine. This is the patent for the paper-rewind mechanism to the tabulator. Davidson graduated from Howard University in 1893.

INVENTIONS, MODIFICATIONS, AND PATENTS

Thomas L. Jennings	Dry-cleaning process	March 1821
Henry Blair	Corn planter	October 1834
Henry Blair	Cotton planter	August 1836
Norbert Rillieux	Sugar refining machine	1843
J. Hawkins	Gridiron design	March 1845
Norbert Rillieux	Sugar refiner	December 1846
Louis Temple	Toggle harpoon	circa 1848
James Forten	Sail control	circa 1850
Sarah E. Goode	Folding cabinet bed	1858
H. Lee	Animal trap design	February 1867
W. A. Deitz	Shoe design	April 1867
T. Elkins	Dining/ironing table/ quilting frame combined	February 1870
J. W. West	Wagon design	October 1870
H. Spears	Portable infantry shield	December 1870

L. Bell	Train smokestack	May 1871
T. Elkins	Chamber commode	January 1872
T. J. Byrd	Horse reins	February 1872
T. J. Byrd	Horse and carriage device	March 1872
T. J. Byrd	Horse yoke design	April 1872
T. J. Marshall	Fire extinguisher design	May 1872
Elijah McCoy	Lubricating system for steam engines	July 1872
L. Bell	Dough kneader	December 1872
Elijah McCoy	Lubricator	May 1873
Lewis Howard Latimer and Brown	Train car water closet	February 1874
E. H. Sutton	Cotton cultivator	April 1874
Elijah McCoy	Ironing table	May 1874
H. Pickett	Scaffold design	June 1874
T. J. Byrd	Train coupling design	December 1874
D. A. Fisher	Joiners' clamp	April 1875
A. P. Ashbourne	Coconut prep process	June 1875
H. H. Nash	Life preserving stool	October 1875
A. P. Ashbourne	Biscuit cutter	November 1875
D. A. Fisher	Furniture castor	March 1876
T. A. Carrington	Range	July 1876
A. P. Ashbourne	Coconut-treating process	August 1877
B. H. Taylor	Rotary engine design	April 1878
J. B. Winters	Fire escape ladder design	May 1878
W. R. Davis, Jr.	Library table	September 1878

Inventions, Modifications, and Patents

W. A. Lavalette	Printing press design	September 1878
O. Dorsey	Door-handling device	December 1878
M. W. Binga	Street-sprinkling apparatus	July 1879
William Bailes	Ladder scaffolding support	August 1879
T. Elkins	Refrigerating device	November 1879
S. R. Scottron	Adjustable window cornice	February 1880
J. N. Waller	Shoemaker's cabinet	February 1880
A. P. Ashbourne	Coconut oil refining process	July 1880
T. B. Pinn	File holder design	August 1880
P. Johnson	Eye protector	November 1880
J. Wormley	Lifesaving apparatus	May 1881
W. S. Campbell	Self-setting animal trap	August 1881
Lewis Howard Latimer and Joseph V. Nichols	Electric lamp	September 1881
P. Johnson	Swinging chairs design	November 1881
Lewis Howard Latimer and Tregoning	Globe support for electric lamp	March 1882
E. Little	Bridle bit design	March 1882
A. C. Richardson	Hame fastener	March 1882
W. B. Purvis	Bag fastener	April 1882
Lewis Howard Latimer	Manufacturing carbons	June 1882
S. R. Scottron	Cornice	January 1883
W. B. Purvis	Hand stamp	February 1883

H. H. Reynolds	Railway window ventilator	April 1883
J. Cooper	Shutter and fastening	May 1883
W. Washington	Corn-husking machine	August 1883
L. C. Bailey	Combination truss and bandage	September 1883
S. E. Thomas	Waste trap	October 1883
C. L. Mitchell	Phneterisin	January 1884
W. Johnson	Eggbeater	February 1884
L. Blue	Corn-shelling device	May 1884
Granville T. Woods	Steam boiler furnace	June 1884
T. S. Church	Carpet-beating machine	July 1884
J. W. Reed	Dough kneader and roller	September 1884
Granville T. Woods	Telephone transmitter	December 1884
John P. Parker	Tobacco press screw	1884
G. T. Sampson	Sled propeller	February 1885
W. F. Cosgrove	Automatic stop plug for gas oil pipes	March 1885
Granville T. Woods	Apparatus for transmission of messages by electricity	April 1885
Elijah McCoy	Steam dome	June 1885
Sarah E. Goode	Folding cabinet bed	July 1885
W. C. Carter	Umbrella stand	August 1885
Lewis Howard Latimer	Apparatus for disinfecting and cooling	January 1886
R. F. Fleming, Jr.	Guitar design	March 1886
J. Ricks	Horseshoe design	March 1886
W. Marshall	Grain binder	May 1886
W. H. Richardson	Cotton chopper	June 1886

Inventions, Modifications, and Patents

W. D. Davis	Riding saddles	October 1896
M. Headen	Foot power hammer	October 1886
Henry Brown	Paper storer	November 1886
I. D. Davis	Tonic	November 1886
J. Robinson	Dinner pail	February 1886
Jan Matzeliger	Shoe-making machine	1886
E. W. Stewart	Machine for making vehicle seat bars	March 1887
J. Gregory	Motor design	April 1887
Elijah McCoy	Lubricator attachment	April 1887
E. R. Lewis	Spring gun	May 1887
Elijah McCoy	Safety valve lubricator	May 1887
D. W. Shorter	Feed rack	May 1887
E. W. Stewart	Punching machine	May 1887
Granville T. Woods	Relay instrument	June 1887
Granville T. Woods	Polarized relay	July 1887
Granville T. Woods	Electromechanical brake	August 1887
R. Hawkins	Harness attachment	October 1887
A. Miles	Elevator concept	October 1887
Granville T. Woods	Phone system and apparatus	October 1887
Granville T. Woods	Railway telegraphy	November 1887
Granville T. Woods	Induction telegraph system	November 1887
Stewart and Johnson	Metal bending machine	December 1887
A. B. Blackburn	Railway signal	January 1888
D. Johnson	Rotary dining table	January 1888
A. B. Blackburn	Spring seat for chairs	April 1888
M. A. Cherry	Velocipede design	May 1888

Granville T. Woods	Overhead conducting system for electric trains	May 1888
Granville T. Woods	Electromotive train system	June 1888
Miriam E. Benjamin	Gong/signal chair	July 1888
Granville T. Woods	Galvanic battery	August 1888
A. B. Blackburn	Cash carrier	October 1888
O. B. Claire	Trestle design	October 1888
P. W. Cornwall	Draft regulator	October 1888
S. E. Thomas	Pipe connection design	October 1888
J. S. Coolidge	Harness attachment	November 1888
R. N. Hyde	Carpet cleaner formula	November 1888
H. Creamer	Steam trap feeder	December 1888
W. A. Johnson	Paint vehicle	December 1888
Frank Winn	Direct acting steam engine	December 1888
Granville T. Woods	Automatic safety cut-out for electric circuits	January 1889
H. Peterson	Lawn mower attachment	April 1889
A. Romain	Passenger register	April 1889
Purdy and Sadgwar	Folding chair design	June 1889
W. H. Richardson	Child's carriage	June 1889
W. A. Martin	Lock design	July 1889
D. Johnson	Lawn mower attachment	September 1889
J. Standard	Oil stove design	October 1889
Elijah McCoy and Hodges	Lubricator	December 1889

Inventions, Modifications, and Patents

W. B. Purvis	Fountain pen	January 1890
F. J. Ferrell	Steam trap	February 1890
Jan Matzeliger	Tack-separating mechanism	March 1890
H. Faulkner	Ventilated shoe	April 1890
F. J. Ferrell	Snow-melting device	May 1890
P. B. Downing	Electric railroad switch	June 1890
D. Johnson	Lawn mower grass catcher	June 1890
A. Pugsley	Blind stop	July 1890
A. F. Hilyer	Water evaporator attachment for hot-air register	August 1890
J. W. Benton	Derrick for hoisting	October 1890
H. H. Reynolds	Safety gate for bridges	October 1890
Snow and Johns	Liniment formula	October 1890
Isaac Watkins	Scrubbing frame	October 1890
D. McCree	Portable fire escape	November 1890
W. Murray	Attachment for bicycles	January 1891
P. D. Smith	Potato digger	January 1891
A. C. Richardson	Churn design	February 1891
W. B. Abrams	Hame attachment	April 1891
G. Toliver	Propeller design	April 1891
J. Standard	Refrigerator design	July 1891
W. Queen	Guard for companionways and hatches	August 1891
H. Linden	Piano truck	September 1891
Jan Matzeliger	Shoe-lasting machine	September 1891
Elijah McCoy	Drip cup	September 1891

P. B. Downing	Letter box design	October 1891
Granville T. Woods	Electric railway system	November 1891
Henry A. Bowman	Flag-making technique	February 1892
F. R. Perryman	Caterers' tray table	February 1892
P. D. Smith	Grain binder	February 1892
C. Williams	Canopy frame	February 1892
Sarah Boone	Ironing board	April 1892
R. Coates	Overboot design for horses	April 1892
G. T. Sampson	Clothes dryer	June 1892
Andrew Jackson Beard	Rotary engine	July 1892
O. E. Brown	Horseshoe design	August 1892
S. R. Scottron	Curtain rod	August 1892
A. L. Lewis	Window cleaner	September 1892
G. E. Becket	Letter box design	October 1892
L. F. Brown	Bridle bit	October 1892
F. J. Loudin	Sash fastener	December 1892
P. W. Cornwall	Draft regulator	February 1893
J. R. Watts	Bracket for miners' lamp	March 1893
L. W. Benjamin	Broom moistener and bridle	May 1893
T. W. Stewart	Mop design	June 1893
T. W. Stewart	Station indicator	June 1893
E. R. Robinson	Electric trolley design	September 1893
C. B. Brooks	Punch	October 1893
F. J. Loudin	Key fastener	January 1894
G. W. Murray	Furrow opener/stalk knocker	April 1894

Inventions, Modifications, and Patents

G. W. Murray	Cultivator and marker	April 1894
S. Newson	Oil heater and cooker	May 1894
G. W. Murray	Planter design	June 1894
G. W. Murray	Cotton chopper	June 1894
G. W. Murray	Fertilizer distributor	June 1894
G. W. Murray	Combined cotton seed	June 1894
R. H. Gray	Baling press	August 1894
Joseph Lee	Bread-kneading machine	August 1894
A. C. Richardson	Casket-lowering device	November 1894
M. A. Cherry	Streetcar fender	January 1895
J. T. Dawkins	Ventilation aid	February 1895
H. Creamer	Steam feed water trap design	March 1895
C. J. Dorticus	Shoe-dying device	March 1895
J. Cooper	Elevator device	April 1895
C. J. Dorticus	Photo print wash	April 1895
C. J. Dorticus	Photo-embossing machine	April 1895
R. H. Gray	Cistern cleaners	April 1895
Purdy and Peters	Design for spoons	April 1895
W. B. Purvis	Magnetic car-balancing device	May 1895
Joseph Lee	Bread-crumbing machine	June 1895
J. L. Love	Plasterers' hawk	July 1895
L. A. Russell	Guard attachment for beds	August 1895
E. H. Holmes	Gauge design	November 1895
J. B. Allen	Clothesline support	December 1895
W. D. Davis	Riding saddles	1896

H. Grenon	Razor-stropping device	February 1896
William H. Johnson	Overcoming "dead centers"	February 1896
Jan Matzeliger	Shoe-nailing machine	February 1896
C. B. Brooks	Street sweepers	March 1896
Lewis Howard Latimer	Locking coat-and hatrack	March 1896
D. N. Roster	Feather curler	March 1896
A. J. Polk	Bicycle support	April 1896
W. S. Grant	Curtain rod support	August 1896
O'Conner and Turner	Alarm for boilers	August 1896
O'Conner and Turner	Steam gauge design	August 1896
H. A. Jackson	Kitchen table design	October 1896
K. Morehead	Reel carrier	October 1896
W. Purdy	Tool sharpener	October 1896
Granville T. Woods	Electricity distribution system	October 1896
J. H. Hunter	Portable weighing scales	November 1896
J. F. Hammonds	Yarn holder design	December 1896
J. T. White	Lemon squeezer	December 1896
D. L. White	Car extension steps	January 1897
A. L. Cralle	Ice-cream mold	February 1897
P. Walker	Machine for cleaning seed cotton	February 1897
J. H. Dunnington	Horse detatchers	March 1897
W. H. Jackson	Railway switch design	March 1897
W. U. Moody	Game board design	May 1897
W. H. Phelps	Vehicle washing apparatus	May 1897
J. W. Smith	Lawn sprinkler design	May 1897

Inventions, Modifications, and Patents

R. A. Butler	Train alarm	June 1897
C. V. Richey	Car-coupling design	June 1897
T. H. Edmonds	Separating screens	July 1897
B. H. Taylor	Slide valve	July 1897
W. B. Purvis	Electric railway switch	August 1897
L. P. Ray	Dust pan	August 1897
C. V. Richey	Railway switch design	August 1897
J. H. Haines	Portable basin	September 1897
F. W. Leslie	Envelope seal design	September 1897
J. H. Evans	Convertible settees	October 1897
Andrew Jackson Beard	Train car coupler	November 1897
J. L. Love	Pencil sharpener	November 1897
E. R. Robinson	Casting composite	November 1897
J. A. Sweeting	Cigarette-rolling device	November 1897
C. V. Richey	Fire escape bracket	December 1897
R. Hearness	Bottle cap design	February 1898
A. L. Rickman	Overshoe	February 1898
W. J. Ballow	Combined hatrack/ table	March 1898
Benjamin F. Jackson	Heating apparatus	March 1898
P. Walker	Bait holder	March 1898
J. A. Joyce	Ore bucket	April 1898
Benjamin F. Jackson	Matrix drying apparatus	May 1898
A. L. Ross	Bag closure	June 1898
J. A. Sweeting	Knife/scoop design	June 1898

G.A.E. Barnes	Sign design	August 1898
W. H. Jackson	Automatic locking switch	August 1898
Jones and Long	Bottle cap	September 1898
C. O. Bailiff	Shampoo headrest	October 1898
C. W. Allen	Self-leveling table	November 1898
F. H. Harding	Extension banquet table	November 1898
Elijah McCoy	Oil cup	November 1898
L. D. Newman	Brush design	November 1898
J. W. Outlaw	Horseshoe design	November 1898
C. V. Richey	Hammock-stretcher	December 1898
J. H. Dickenson	Pianola	1899
E. P. Ray	Chair-supporting device	February 1899
A. C. Richardson	Insect "destroyer"	February 1899
L. F. Booker	Rubber scraping knife	March 1899
J. H. Robinson	Train safety guard	March 1899
Benjamin F. Jackson	Gas burner	April 1899
J. A. Burr	Lawn mower	May 1899
G. Cook	Automatic fishing device	May 1899
R. R. Reynolds	Nonrefillable bottle	May 1899
F. W. Griffin	Pool table attachment	June 1899
W. Johnson	Velocipede design	June 1899
W. J. Nickerson	Mandolin and guitar attachment for pianos	June 1899
J. Ricks	Overshoes for horses	June 1899
L. C. Bailey	Folding bed	July 1899

Inventions, Modifications, and Patents

B. F. Cargill	Invalid cot	July 1899
C. J. Dorticus	Hose leak stopper	July 1899
R. Hearness	Detachable car fender	July 1899
A. R. Cooper	Shoemaker's jack	August 1899
Elijah McCoy	Lawn sprinkler system	September 1899
J. Ross	Baling press	September 1899
E. H. West	Weather shield	September 1899
W. F. Burr	Railway switching device	October 1899
J. W. Butts	Luggage carrier	October 1899
I. R. Johnson	Bicycle frame	October 1899
J. P. Williams	Pillow sham holder	October 1899
W. Burwell	Boot or shoe	November 1899
Jan Matzeliger	Tack-distributing mechanism	November 1899
A. Mendenhall	Holder for driving reins	November 1899
A. L. Ross	Trousers support	November 1899
George F. Grant	Golf tee	December 1899
J. M. Certain	Parcel carrier for bike	December 1899
J. B. Rhodes	Water closet design	December 1899
A. C. Richardson	Bottle design	December 1899
S. W. Gunn	Boot/shoe design	January 1900
J. M. Mitchell	Corn planter design	January 1900
J. F. Pickering	Airship	February 1900
Madame C. J. Walker	Hot comb	1900

Granville T. Woods	Regulating and controlling electrical translating devices	September 1901
Granville T. Woods	Automatic air brake	June 1902
Lewis Howard Latimer	Book supports	February 1905
Richard B. Spikes	Locking billiard cue rack	circa 1910
Lewis Howard Latimer	Lamp fixture	August 1910
Frederick M. Johnson	Self-feeding rapid-fire rifle	circa 1912
Garrett Augustus Morgan	Gas mask	1914
Hubert Julian	Airplane safety device	May 1921
Garrett Augustus Morgan	Traffic light	1923
William Hale	Airplane improvement	April 1925
Richard B. Spikes	Milk bottle opener/ cover	June 1926
Marjorie Joyner	Hair wave machine	1928
Solomon Harper	Electric hair treatment	August 1930
Percy L. Julian	Glaucoma drug	circa 1931
Richard B. Spikes	Method and apparatus for obtaining average samples and temperature of tank liquids	October 1931
Richard B. Spikes	Automatic gearshift design	December 1932
Lloyd Augustus Hall	Sterilizing foodstuff	February 1938
Richard B. Spikes	Automatic shoeshine chair	circa 1939

Inventions, Modifications, and Patents

Frederick M. Jones	Movie ticket machine	June 1939
Richard B. Spikes	Multiple-barrel machine gun	circa 1940
Charles R. Drew	Blood plasma storage	circa 1940
Percy Julian	Recovery of sterols	October 1940
Joseph Blair	Speedboat design	1942
Lloyd Augustus Hall	Puncture-sealing mixture	September 1944
Joseph Blair	Aerial torpedo design	1944
Frederick M. Jones	Two-cycle gasoline engine	May 1945
Lloyd Augustus Hall	Preserving process	March 1949
Frederick M. Jones	Air conditioner design	July 1949
Frederick M. Jones	Starter generator for cooling gas engines	July 1949
Frederick M. Jones	Rotary compressor	April 1950
Frederick M. Jones	Refrigeration unit design	May 1950
Frederick M. Jones	Two-cycle gasoline engine	November 1950
Frederick M. Jones	Refrigerator construction design	December 1950
G. S. Bluford, Sr.	Artillery ammunition training round	February 1951
Solomon Harper	Thermostatic control hair curlers	August 1953
Frederick M. Jones	Defrosting method	January 1954
Percy L. Julian	Preparation of cortisone	August 1954
Frederick M. Jones	Air-conditioning method	December 1954
Frederick M. Jones	Combustion-engine device	September 1958

Robert Bundy	Signal generator design	January 1960
Frederick M. Jones	Thermostat design	February 1960
Betsy Ancker Johnson	Signal generator design	November 1966
Paul Brown	Wiz-z-zer spinning top	1968
M. C. Gourdine	Electrogas dynamic apparatus	June 1969
George R. Carruthers	Ultraviolet spectrograph	November 1969
Bayliss and Emrick	Encapsulation process	February 1971
Earl Shaw	Spin fly tunable laser	1972
Al Prather	Man-powered glider aircraft	February 1973
Christian Reeburg	Grease gun stand	August 1978
Richard L. Saxton	Tissue dispenser for phone booth	February 1981
Carter, Weiner, Youmans	Distributed pulse-forming network for magnetic modulator	September 1986
Dixon, AuCoin, Malik	Monolithic planar doped barrier	March 1987

INDEX

Page numbers in *italics* refer to illustrations.

199

Index